designed by God

Answers to Students' Questions About Homosexuality

Pam Gibbs

LifeWay Press ®
Nashville, Tennessee

Published by LifeWay Press®

© Copyright 2004

ISBN: 0-6330-9865-5

Dewey Decimal Classification Number: 306.78
Subject Heading: SEXUAL BEHAVIOR \ HOMOSEXUALITY

Printed in the United States of America

Student Ministry Publishing
LifeWay Church Resources
One LifeWay Plaza
Nashville, Tennessee 37234-0174

CONTENTS

How to Use this Book

You've probably picked up this book for a reason. Maybe you've read a lot of controversy about homosexuality in the newspapers or heard about it on TV. You may have heard a lecture at school that said homosexuality should be celebrated and accepted. You might have questions about what the Bible really says about homosexuality. Or, like lots of other teenagers, you may be struggling with feelings of homosexuality. In any case, this book is designed to help you answer some common questions about homosexuality.

Hopefully, this study will help you find some answers. You can work through this book by yourself. Take a few minutes each day to read and reflect on the things you learn. Work at your own pace. Take as much time as you need. It might be helpful to find a quiet place where you can read and work through the book without any interruptions—your bedroom, a hammock out back, a library, or even a bookstore coffee shop. Don't forget to bring your Bible along!

You can also work through this study with a group of friends at church. Encourage your youth worker to help you complete the study. (There are some pages in the back of the book for a small-group discussion.) If you use this as a group study, be sure to bring your book each week. Complete the activities as assigned and participate in the discussion. You'll learn a lot from others, and others can learn from you, too.

ORIGINAL DESIGN
How Did God Design Men and Women to Relate to Each Other?

I am gay. Perhaps you've heard this statement before. Maybe in a moment of struggle, one of your friends whispered the words to you. Or maybe you've thought it yourself. You've watched talk shows about it. Seen movies about it. Heard about it in the news, or read about it in the paper. The truth is homosexuality has become commonplace in our world today, maybe even more so in your world as a teenager.

What are some things you've heard about homosexuality? Think about things you've read in magazines or things you've watched on TV or in movies. _____
_____
_____
_____
_____

If you're like many teenagers, you have a lot of questions about homosexuality and want some honest answers. Hopefully, this book will provide some answers. Over the next few pages, you'll learn what God's Word says about homosexuality. You'll discover God's original design for us as men and women. You'll learn how things got messed up so badly. You'll uncover the lies culture has fed you about homosexuality, and you'll discover how to respond to friends or family members who are convinced that they are gay. You'll also learn how to develop healthy, God-honoring relationships.

Throughout these pages, I hope you'll discover one central truth: God loves you. He created you and everyone around you uniquely and wonderfully—with gifts, character traits, and emotions that are to be celebrated and used to honor Him.

Let's get started on this journey of learning about God's design.

Design Is Everywhere

As you're sitting here reading the words on this pages, stop and think about what had to happen to get these words from the writer's brain onto the paper you're now holding in your hands. What steps occurred in this process? _____

_____

_____

_____

_____

_____

You probably thought about the words being printed on the pages with ink, the pages being bound together with a staple on some massive assembly line. You may have even thought about the delivery trucks or the salesperson at the store. But there's much more involved. In fact, writing begins with one major thing: design. A writer has a design in mind when he or she begins a project. He or she will think about the number of chapters, the order or sequence of those chapters, and the intended outcome of each idea in the book. What would a book be like without any design? It would just be a garbled mess of words without any purpose or direction.

If you think about it, lots of other things in our world are based on a specific design. Just look around the room and notice things that have a specific design. List some of them in the space provided. _____

_____

_____

_____

_____

_____

Maybe you're sitting in a chair as you read this. That chair was designed by someone to look and feel a specific way and serve a specific purpose: allowing you to sit comfortably. Check out the shoes you're wearing. They were created with a specific kind of material, measured to be a specific size and weight, and formed to fit your foot's arch in all the right places.

Design is all around you, and it's even in your body. Your white blood cells are designed to defend the body against infectious diseases and foreign materials. Your pancreas digests fats and proteins, and your nose hair actually catches airborne particles and keeps them from reaching the lungs (gross, but true!). Just as different body parts are created with a design, God created your sexuality with a specific design. Where can you learn more about God's design for your sexuality? Let's go to Genesis, the first book of the Bible, to find that answer.

Back to the Beginning— Created Male and Female

If you've never read Genesis 1, take a few minutes now to do so.

What happens in the first chapter of the Bible? Creation. God created the world and everything in it. He created it all—from the spotted owl to the Grand Tetons to the galaxy we call the Milky Way. And Scripture tells us that God called His creation good (Gen. 1:10,18,25,31). In the midst of this creation chapter, the writer also explained the creation of humanity.

Read Genesis 1:26-28.

What makes humanity different from the rest of creation?

_____

_____

_____

_____

_____

_____

What does it mean to be created in God's image? _____

_____

_____

_____

_____

Why is it important that God created humanity "male and female"? _____

_____

_____

_____

What commands did God give the man and woman?

_____

_____

_____

_____

In the very first chapter of the Bible, we learn a lot about our design as human beings. First, the Bible tells us that we were created in God's image. Since God is spirit, we don't resemble Him physically, but we are like Him in other ways. Like Him, we have the ability to be creative. We experience emotions, just as God does (Gen. 6:6; Matt. 26:38). Most importantly, though, we can share in a personal relationship with Him.

Second, this passage tells us that men and women are made as unique creations. God didn't set forth one gender of humanity. He created men, and He created women—two distinct genders. Obviously, each gender is physically different, but men and women often experience emotions differently, think differently, and relate to others differently. There's nothing wrong with that—we're just different. God said those differences were good (Gen. 1:31).

How do you feel knowing that God created men and women to be different? _____

_____

_____

How have you experienced or seen the differences between men and women?

_____

_____

Do you like being created differently from the opposite sex? Why or why not?

_____

_____

_____

Back to the Beginning—Created to Relate

While the first chapter of Genesis gives us the big picture of all of creation, the second chapter of Genesis provides more information for us.

Read Genesis 2:18-25.

What do we learn about creation in verse 19? _____

_____

_____

What was Adam's job? _____

_____

_____

What does verse 20 tell us about all of these creatures Adam named? _____

_____

_____

How did God create woman? What is unique about this creation?

_____

_____

_____

Why did He create the woman? _____

_____

_____

What was Adam's reaction to this new creation? _____

_____

_____

Reread Genesis 2:24 and rewrite it in your own words.

_____

_____

_____

The Story Unfolded

This story provides a great framework for understanding our sexual design as men and women. Let's review a bit. God created all of the animals and brought them before Adam for him to choose a name for each of them. And that's just what Adam did. Scripture tells us that among all of those creatures, no "suitable helper" could be found for Adam. In other words, although it was not good for man to be alone (v. 18), none of the animals could provide what Adam needed in a relationship. So God put Adam into a deep sleep and took one of his ribs. From that rib God fashioned a woman—a person who could relate to Adam emotionally, spiritually, and sexually. In creating Eve as the complement, partner, and helper to Adam, God set forth the framework for biblical sexuality: between one man and one woman within the boundaries of marriage. Notice that God didn't create another male to be a helper. He created a woman, someone distinctly different from the man.

Notice the beautiful picture in verse 24: "This is why a man leaves his father and mother and bonds with his wife, and they become one flesh." This verse describes the heterosexual union of a man and woman as God set forth when He created them. But the word *flesh* doesn't just refer to physical union through sexual intercourse. To the Greeks and Hebrews (the original languages of the Bible), the word *flesh* referred to the whole human being. In other words, sex as God designed it doesn't just join two people physically; it is an act that joins their emotions and spirits as well. A husband and wife create a bond that is much deeper than physical attraction or sexual gratification—a bond that is not easily broken and is painful when destroyed.

Putting It All Together

In Genesis, God set forth the plan for how men and women should relate to each other. God created men and women to be united together within the bounds of marriage. Throughout the Bible, God confirmed the importance of this plan (Song of Sol; Heb. 13:4). It is important to note that in Scripture, there is no positive reference to homosexuality—it's not how God designed people to relate to each other. On the other hand, Scripture is full of instructions about how men and women are to treat each other within a marriage relationship (1 Cor. 6:18-20; Eph. 5:22-33; Col. 3:18-19).

If God designed sexuality to be expressed between men and women within the boundaries of marriage, then what happened? Why is homosexuality such a struggle for some people? In the next chapter, you'll find out.

Chapter 1 Notes

Chapter 1 Notes

THE FALL
What Happened to God's Plan?

Imagine for a minute that you like to build things. For Christmas you decide to build a huge birdhouse for your mom to put in the backyard. You spend hours measuring the wood, cutting the angles correctly, and hammering the nails at just the right spots. Carefully, you paint the outside and place holes in just the right places for the birds to go in and build nests for the winter. You're proud of your creation. You wrap up your gift and put it underneath the tree. On Christmas day your mother opens the gift and beams with pride. "It's beautiful! The birds will love it! It'll be so nice to look out the kitchen window and watch birds building their nests," she exclaims. She loves her Christmas gift!

About a week later, while taking the trash outside, you notice something strange. Your mom is in the backyard—with an axe in her hand. Then you see it. Your birdhouse. Before you can say anything, your mom swings the axe, splitting through the wood and smashing the birdhouse to pieces. Just then she looks up and says, "Oh, hi. Thanks again for the birdhouse. It'll make great kindling for the fireplace."

You're devastated. How could your mom destroy something you made for her? You spent countless hours crafting a present your mom would love and enjoy. But she destroyed it. It was never meant to start a fire. It was meant for a much greater purpose.

Of course, this story is fiction. No mother would destroy something given in love. She would cherish it and watch birds build their nests in it.

The story is an illustration of sin. God has created us uniquely and beautifully, an act of love and creativity much like building the birdhouse. However, we choose not to live as God designed. We sin against Him and destroy our lives in the process, just as the mother destroyed the birdhouse. But how did sin enter the picture? Let's discover where the problems began.

Read Genesis 3:1-13.

Listed below are the events found in the verses you just read. However, they're in the wrong order. Put them back in order by putting a number 1 by the first thing that happened, the number 2 by the next thing, and so forth.

___ They sewed fig leaves together and made coverings for themselves.

___ Eve blamed the serpent for her decision to sin against God.

___ The serpent questioned whether God had really told Adam and Eve not to eat from any tree in the garden.

___ The woman gave the fruit to her husband who was with her, and he ate it, too.

___ The man and woman hid from God when He came to the garden looking for them.

___ Eve said that she and Adam could eat any tree from the garden except for the one in the middle of the garden.

___ The woman ate the fruit.

___ Adam and Eve realized they were naked.

___ The woman saw that the fruit was good for food, pretty, and could provide wisdom.

___ God called out for Adam and Eve.

___ The serpent said God didn't want Adam and Eve to eat the forbidden food because He didn't want them to be like Him.

___ Adam blamed Eve for his decision to sin against God.

___ The serpent told the woman she wouldn't die from eating the fruit from the forbidden tree.

Reviewing a Tragic Story

Let's review the story. Scripture tells us in verse 1 that the serpent was craftier than any other creature in the garden.

How would you define *crafty*? _____

_____

_____

What did the serpent say or do that was crafty? _____

_____

_____

When the serpent came to Eve, he didn't use tactics that would make her suspicious of his motives. He was deceptive. He called into question God's commands. He asked Eve, "Did God really say…?" In other words, he was trying to lure the creation away from the Creator, making God's law seem unclear or unreasonable. He was drawing Eve away from the truth using doubt and ill-formed logic.

His deceptive tricks worked. Eve began to listen to him, and he filled her mind with lies. In fact, he boldly stated, "You will not die." This statement is in direct opposition to God's stated consequences for rebellion. (See Gen. 2:17.) Then he told her another lie—that God didn't want Adam and Eve to eat the fruit because He didn't want them to be like Him, knowing good and evil.

Eve took the bait, and she ate the fruit. She gave it to Adam, and he ate it also. In that one moment sin entered the realm of human existence. Ever wonder why things are so evil and crazy in the world today? You can trace the roots to this one event. The man and woman, created by God to glorify Him and live in communion with Him, had existed in sinless perfection until this moment in history. They deliberately chose their own will instead of God's perfect plan. The effects of sin were immediate.

What happened when Adam and Eve ate the fruit? What did they realize? _____

_____

_____

In the moment that the man and woman rebelled against God, Adam and Eve realized they were naked. In an effort to cover their bodies and their embarrassment, they sewed fig leaves together for clothing. (Can you imagine how uncomfortable that must have been?) But the coverings for their bodies couldn't hide the sin in their hearts.

In fact, when God came looking for them, what did they do?

_____

_____

_____

How did God respond to them? _____

_____

_____

How do you think God felt in that moment when He saw that Adam and Eve had rebelled against Him? _____

_____

_____

When God confronted Adam and Eve, He asked them a question: "Did you eat fruit from the tree from which I told you not to eat?" Guess what both Adam and Eve said in response? It was somebody else's fault! Adam blamed Eve, and Eve blamed the serpent, but it was too late. Sin had entered the picture, and the world was forever changed. (Read Genesis 3:14-24 to learn what happened to Adam and Eve.)

Putting the Pieces Together

So what does this story have to do with homosexuality? Glad you asked. Before Adam and Eve sinned, they lived as God had originally designed—in sinless perfection and in communion with Him and each other. When sin entered the picture, humanity began to live outside the boundaries of God's perfect plan, seeking and fulfilling their own desires. In fact, in the next chapter of Genesis, a murder took place. By chapter 6, the whole world was full of evil. Genesis 6:5 states that every inclination of humanity's heart was only evil all the time. Ever since Adam and Eve's decision to eat from the tree, humans have been living in sinful rebellion against God.

One of the ways people rebel against God is by engaging in homosexual behavior. They warp God's original plan for their sexuality—sexual intimacy between one man and one woman within the boundaries of marriage—and think that they can fulfill their God-given sexual desires in some other way. Like Adam and Eve, people involved in homosexual behavior often try to blame someone or something else for their sinful actions, even stating that God made them gay, so they have the freedom to express their "God-given" urges. Like the serpent, they question God's command—did God REALLY say homosexuality was sinful? In asking this question, they try to change God's Word to justify their behavior.

Remember, though, that homosexuality is only one way people rebel against God. Committing adultery is also a sin; so is lusting. Lying, gluttony (overeating), and prejudice are all examples of sin. And just like those who struggle with homosexuality, people caught in any other sin often try to blame others—"I committed adultery because living with my wife is horrible" or "I couldn't help but lust after her. Did you see the way she was dressed?" or "I only lied to protect her from being hurt." Scripture tells us that every person who has ever lived (except for Jesus Christ) has sinned. To say we have not sinned is simply a lie.

Read Romans 3:23.

What does this verse tell us about every person? _____

_____

_____

_____

Read 1 John 1:8-10.

What do these verses say about every person? _____

_____

_____

Bad News, Good News

That's the bad news. We've all sinned. We've all rebelled against God. And because of our rebellion, we experience the consequences of sin. However, there's good news. God loved us too much to leave us in our sinful condition.

Read Romans 6:23.

What is the penalty for our sin? _____

_____

_____

What is the gift of God? _____

_____

_____

Where is this eternal life found? _____

_____

This verse makes clear that the payment of sin—what we "earn" or the consequences of choosing to sin—is death. Does that mean the penalty of sin is physical death? Well, yes. Part of sin's effect in our world concerns our physical bodies. We are weak—susceptible to disease, sickness, and aging. The end result for all of us will be physical death. But sin's most devastating consequence is spiritual death—eternal separation from God. He is perfect and holy and because of sin, we are not. Therefore, we are separated from Him. We are separated from the One who created us and loves us more than we could ever comprehend. But God's love compelled Him to provide a way out for us, a solution to our sin problem. Romans 6:23 tells us that we can have eternal life with God through Jesus Christ.

Read Romans 5:8 and rewrite it in your own words.

_____

_____

_____

Here's the good news. While we were still separated from God because of our sin, Christ died for us. Even though we were supposed to die for our sins (remember Rom. 6:23 that you just read?), Jesus died in our place. In fact, He was crucified (see John 19:1-30). But Scripture also tells us that He rose from the dead, conquering death itself, and is alive today (see John 20:1-9).

Read John 3:16 and Romans 10:9-10,13.

According to John 3:16, why did God send His son? _____

_____

_____

_____

What do these verses say is necessary for us to be saved?

_____

_____

_____

_____

According to these verses, who can be saved from sin? _____

_____

_____

_____

What do we receive as a result of trusting in Jesus Christ as our Savior? _____

_____

_____

_____

John 3:16 states that God loved you and me so much that He sent His Son to earth. Romans 10:9-10,13 tells us that when we place our trust in Jesus Christ, we are saved. Anyone who chooses to turn from sin and puts his or her faith in Christ can have eternal life. If you've never turned from your sin to faith in Christ, it's not too late. God loves you and wants you to have the life for which you were created—a life of communion with Him, a life of trust and obedience that results in the life He designed for you. As a believer, your life is lived with Him as Lord, directing and guiding your life. If you have more questions about what it means to be a Christian, talk to your youth minister or pastor.

Equal Footing

If you've spent much time in a large metropolitan area, you know that the buildings can be quite an amazing sight. Walking down the streets of New York City, for example, you'll gaze up at buildings that seem to reach the sky. (In fact, on foggy days, you cannot see the tops of those buildings!) Beside the tall skyscrapers are buildings that are just a few stories tall. Standing side by side, you can easily judge the differences in size and shape of two different office complexes. However, if you take a plane trip over that same city, things will look quite differently. You'll no longer be able to tell the difference between a 12-story building and a 100-story building. Why?

Because your viewpoint has changed. Your perspective is above the buildings, not eye-level with them. They're all just buildings.

It's the same way with sin. People measure sin differently than God does. You and I tend to judge one sin as worse or better than another. We think that our sin of lying isn't nearly as horrible as someone else's sin of adultery. For some people, the sin of adultery isn't as bad as the sin of homosexuality. Others feel just the opposite. For many, homosexuality ranks as one of those "100-story" sins. However, from God's perspective, sin is sin. There's no measurement to it, no ranking from really big to minor or insignificant. Anything that rebels against God's commands is sin. It's true that different kinds of sin carry different consequences. A teenage girl who engages in premarital sex may be infected with a disease. A man with poor eating habits faces high blood pressure and possibly premature death. While the consequences may differ, sin is sin, no matter how it is classified.

How do you feel knowing that your sin is no better and no worse than the sin of others around you? _____

_____

_____

_____

In what ways have you tried to make your sin seem less evil or repulsive than the sin of others? _____

_____

_____

_____

Maybe you've picked up this book because you're struggling with homosexuality and you want answers. This may be the first time you've ever been told that God loves you. Believe it. God loves you deeply and unconditionally. Even though you have sinned against God, He still loves you. In fact, nothing you do will change the fact that He loves you. No matter what other people may say, God does not hate gay people. He loves homosexuals.

However, God loves you too much to allow you to continue to live outside His design. He doesn't prohibit homosexual behavior because He wants you to be miserable and to struggle all your life. He created you and therefore knows what's best for your life. That's why He set forth His commands in the Bible, including the parameters for sexual expression. That's also why He provided commands against lying, murder, and other behaviors. His commands are meant to bring good, not harm.

On the other hand, maybe you've always believed that some sins are worse than others. Perhaps you've been fed the lie that God categorizes sin and punishes the worst sins accordingly. You can't be as bad as other people. You go to church. You're a member of the youth group and even went on a mission trip last summer. You've never done anything really sinful, just the little stuff. This may be difficult to accept, but in relation to your sin, you're no better and no worse than a murderer or a child abuser.

At Jesus' Feet
Read John 8:1-11.

In the space below, record a journal entry about this event written from the perspective of the woman. Include things the woman might have been thinking and feeling. Also jot down what she might have seen, heard, or even smelled.

_____

_____

_____

The teachers of the law (the religious leaders in Jesus' day) were trying to trap Jesus. They brought before Him a woman caught in the act of adultery. According to Jewish law, the woman deserved to be put to death for her sin. If Jesus agreed with the law, then He would condemn the woman to death. If He simply let the woman go, then He he would violate the law.

The issue here wasn't really about adultery. These religious men didn't care about the truth. They just wanted to trick Jesus into doing something wrong. But He knew the hearts of these men and offered a solution with which no one could argue. The one without sin could cast the first stone to kill the woman. Wow! Scripture tells us that these self-righteous men began to leave, oldest first (maybe they'd lived longer and could recognize their sin more readily). They were followed by the younger men until only one person was left standing near the woman—Jesus. He was the one person who could indeed throw a stone because He had not sinned. Only Jesus didn't reach for a stone to give her the punishment due such a sinner. Instead, He reached into the depths of her soul and offered her a way out. He told her to leave her life of sin. His mercy imposed no conditions; He offered her a new life.

Which of the characters are you most like? Are you more like the teachers of the law, the ones who thought they were better than other people because they knew God's Word? Or are you more like the woman caught in sin, knowing that the only way out is through the mercy of Jesus? Explain your thoughts below.

_____

_____

_____

Over the next few chapters, we'll be looking at what our culture says about homosexuality. We'll also discover what God's Word says about it. We'll discuss how to respond to people on all sides of the issue. In the midst of this study, keep one thing in mind: we're all equal before God—equally sinners and equally in need of His mercy, grace, and love.

Chapter 2 Notes

Chapter 2 Notes

A LOUD VOICE
What Does Culture Say About Homosexuality?

Ever heard of an urban legend? If you spend much time on the Internet, you probably know what the term means. An urban legend is a story. It's passed along through e-mails and Internet sites, and people claim that the story is true. Often they cite scholarly sounding sources or make claims like "This really works!" or "This really happened to my neighbor!" The stories sound very believable, only most of the time the stories simply aren't true.

Think you can tell the difference between an urban legend and a true story? Read the following stories. Choose either T (True) or UL (Urban Legend).

T or UL   A New York man who wanted to visit his parents in Texas shipped himself in a wooden cargo crate instead of paying for an airline ticket.[1]

T or UL   If you leave a tooth in a glass of Coca-Cola, the beverage will dissolve the tooth overnight.[2]

T or UL   A man who saved Richard Nixon from drowning asked that no one tell his father because his father would be so unhappy that his son had saved the disliked president.[3]

T or UL   A cigar smoker bought several expensive cigars and had them insured against fire. He smoked all of them and then filed a claim because the cigars had been destroyed by fire. The company paid the claim (after going to court). When the man collected the money, he was arrested for arson.[4]

T or UL   A crystal ball, placed on a home owner's couch, set the couch on fire when sunshine came through a set of windows and through the crystal ball.[5]

T or UL   A large percentage of U.S. currency bears traces of cocaine.[6]

How well do you think you did? If you said that statements 1, 5, and 6 were fact, then you were correct. The rest are urban legends. (Check out the references for more information.)

Why are people quick to believe an urban legend? First, those who spread urban legends sound intelligent. They cite statistics, use real places as backdrops for their stories, and claim personal knowledge of the subject. Second, people believe urban legends because they don't take the time to check out the stories. Most people prefer to assume that a story is true rather than take the time and energy to find out the facts. Third, people are prone to believe urban legends because if you hear something repeated enough times, you begin to believe it's true. If a child is told over and over that he is worthless, he or she will begin to believe the lie. The same applies to urban legends. If an urban legend is passed along enough times and retold to enough of the population, eventually people will begin to believe it.

The reasons people believe urban legends are sometimes the same reasons people believe what culture says about homosexuality. When scientists talk about the biological roots of homosexuality, they sound intelligent. They use lots of statistics and complicated words. Because they are authorities in the medical field, they must know the truth, right? (Not necessarily! Just think, decades ago, many medical doctors endorsed cigarettes.) And just as people don't want to take the time to investigate whether an urban legend is based in fact, many people don't want to take the time to see if these researchers' claims are valid. They would rather accept what someone tells them than to find out the facts for themselves. And people often believe what culture says about homosexuality because they've heard so many lies that they don't know what the truth is. Remember, if you're told a lie enough times, you begin to believe it's true.

This chapter focuses on the messages today's culture is presenting and promoting about homosexuality. We'll examine the scientific studies that researchers have conducted and will evaluate their conclusions. Hopefully, you'll learn to listen critically to the messages you're hearing.

31

Message 1: Homosexuality Is Genetic

Ever hear someone say that homosexuality is genetic? What you heard probably sounds a lot like this:

"Being a homosexual is something you're born with, like your gender or your hair color."

"You can't say it's wrong to be gay when it's been proven that homosexuals are born that way."

"I must have been born this way because I can't fight the feelings I have."

"We need to celebrate the diverse ways God has created us— male, female, homosexual, heterosexual, bisexual, Caucasian, African-American, Asian—instead of judging one another."

"I've been a homosexual since I was young—maybe four or five years old."

The main message behind these types of statements is that homosexuality is genetic. Gay activists and scientists cite scientific studies to show that homosexuality is a genetic tendency or condition with which you're born, not something you choose. Let's take a look at three of those studies to discover researchers' findings and, more importantly, the flaws in those findings.

The X Chromosome Study

In 1993, *Science* magazine released a study done by geneticist Dean Hamer. He and his coworkers studied 40 pairs of brothers who were homosexual, and claimed that 33 of the sets of brothers had inherited the same genetic markers for homosexuality.[7] Hamer claimed to have found a genetic component to homosexuality.[8]

Problems with Hamer's Study

Sounds pretty convincing, doesn't it? When the study came out, it was covered by National Public Radio, *The Wall Street Journal* and *The New York Times*. If these media outlets reported it, then the study must be true, right? Not so fast. Researchers have discovered several problems with this study, but you probably won't hear about those problems in *The Wall Street Journal* or *The New York Times*.

1. This study has not been replicated. One of the basic rules of science is that before being accepted as truth, the results of a scientific study must be reproduced multiple times with the same conclusion. In other words, if I drop an apple from my hand to prove gravity, I must repeatedly drop an apple from my hand to replicate the experiment and prove my hypothesis.

When another group of researchers, including Dr. George Rice and Dr. George Ebers tried to repeat the study of brothers, they found that only about half of the brothers shared the genetic markers. They concluded that "these results are not consistent with an X-linked gene underlying sexual orientation in this region of the X chromosome."[9] In other words, the study wasn't replicated, so it couldn't be proven true.

2. Some of the brothers didn't share the genetic markers that supposedly led to homosexuality. In other words, if a gene is solely responsible for a specific behavior, then that genetic marker should be evident in every instance of homosexuality. Why would a genetic marker NOT show up in every case? In this study, several of the pairs of brothers didn't share a genetic marker for homosexuality. Hamer (the guy who conducted the original experiment) admitted that some origins of homosexuality, namely lesbianism, might be nongenetic.[10] Did you catch that? The scientist who sought to prove that homosexuality is genetic said that in some cases homosexuality might be caused by something *other* than genetics.

The Twin Study

Let's review some basic science before we evaluate another study. What's the difference between fraternal twins and identical twins? Fraternal twins are created from two separate eggs supplied by the woman in reproduction. On the other hand, identical twins are created from one egg from the woman's body. Thus, identical twins share identical genes. That's why identical twins look alike physically.

Two researchers, Michael Bailey and Richard Pillard, conducted a study of pairs of brothers—identical twins, fraternal twins, biological brothers, and adopted brothers. In each case, one of the brothers was a homosexual. The scientists' theory was that identical brothers of homosexual men (who share identical genetic material) would be more likely to be homosexual than other brothers—fraternal, biological, or adopted— who don't share as much genetic material. For example, James and John are identical twins. Richard and Robert are fraternal twins. If James (the identical twin) is a homosexual, then his brother John is more likely to be a homosexual since they share the same genetic codes. Richard and Robert are less likely to both be homosexual because they are fraternal twins (not identical) and do not share any more genes than non-twins.

The study found that over half (52 percent) of the sets of identical twins were both homosexual. Only 22 percent of the sets of fraternal twins were both homosexuals. Researchers concluded that since identical twin brothers share the same genetic codes, then the higher rate of homosexuality among identical twin brothers proved a genetic link for homosexuality.[11] In other words, because the percentage of twins who were both homosexual among identical twins was higher, the researchers determined that homosexuality must be genetic.

Problems with the Twin Study

On the surface this research seems convincing, doesn't it? Look more closely, and you'll see that this study has its faults as well.

1. The findings actually contradict the scientists' theory. Let's break this down logically. Identical twin brothers (or sisters) share the exact genetic code, right? Thus, if homosexuality were solely genetic, then if one twin were homosexual, what would also be true? The other twin would have to be homosexual. Why? Because they share the same genetic code. In other words, the study should have proven that 100 percent of identical homosexual twins would both be homosexual, not just more than half. In trying to prove homosexuality is genetic, the scientists actually showed that genetics alone cannot cause homosexuality. In fact, one of the researchers who headed up the project, Michael Bailey, stated that there must be something in the environment to cause the differences in sexuality between the identical homosexual twins.[12]

2. The brothers in this study were raised in the same household. What difference would this make in disproving the scientists' theory? Maybe an illustration would help explain it. I love watching *Star Trek*. I wasn't born with the genetic codes to make me like *Star Trek*. For years my brother and I would sit in the middle of the living room floor and watch it together. My brother and I don't share a genetic code that made this happen. We were in the same environment and were exposed to the same things.

In the study of homosexual twins, these twins were raised in the same household and experienced many of the same things together. Thus, the fact that both twins are homosexual may have little to do with genetics and more to do with their environment. They may have chosen that behavior because of what happened in their home, not what happened in their genes.

The Hypothalamus Study

Back to our science class for a moment. Your brain is divided into several different parts, and each part performs a different function. For example, the cerebellum coordinates movements of certain muscles, while the pituitary gland regulates growth. Also in your brain is a section called the hypothalamus, which researchers think regulates body temperature, blood pressure, awareness of pleasure and pain, and the expression of emotion, such as rage or fear. It's about the size of an almond.

A scientist named Simon LeVay studied a region of the hypothalamus in 41 cadavers or dead bodies. Of the people he studied, 19 were homosexual men, 16 were heterosexual men, and six were heterosexual women. (At least that's what LeVay concluded about their sexuality. We'll talk about that later.) He found that the region of the hypothalamus he studied was larger in many of the heterosexual men than in homosexuals. He concluded that the hypothalamus was the cause of homosexuality.[13]

Problems with the Hypothalamus Study

1. Which came first? You've heard the old riddle—which came first, the chicken or the egg? In this case, which came first—the smaller hypothalamus or the homosexual behavior? It is impossible to know whether the homosexual behavior changed the brain structure or the brain structure led to the homosexual behavior. In fact, it has been proven that brain structure changes with behavior.[14]

2. His results were not consistent across the board. Remember, he found that in most of the heterosexual men, the hypothalamus was larger. However, three of the homosexual men actually had a LARGER region of the hypothalamus than the heterosexual men. And three of the heterosexual men had SMALLER regions of the hypothalamus than the average homosexual LeVay studied. Did you catch that? Of the 35 men studied, 6 of them contradicted LeVay's theory.[15]

3. LeVay wasn't really certain about the sexuality of the cadavers. Because the men and women he studied were dead, he could only rely on the patients' case studies to tell him whether they were heterosexual or homosexual. If a patient's case study didn't indicate anything, he assumed that person was heterosexual. However, 6 of the 16 men who were supposedly heterosexuals died of AIDS, which increases the likelihood that their sexual histories were incomplete.[16] If he wasn't sure of the patients' sexual behavior, then he would have no way to prove his theory correct.

4. Simon LeVay, the scientist in charge of the study, was biased in his research. Openly homosexual, he once told *Newsweek* magazine after the death of his lover that he was determined to find a genetic cause for homosexuality or "he would abandon the science altogether."[17] His homosexual behavior doesn't make him a bad scientist, but it probably affected his ability to look at the evidence objectively.

Genetics Versus Behavior

Scientists continue to search for a genetic basis for homosexuality. No research has proven such a basis definitively. It's also important to keep in mind that a tendency toward something doesn't make it right. If a teenage boy has a genetic marker for violence, he is not excused to beat up a child or kill a cat. He is still responsible for his choices and his behavior. If my parents were alcoholics, I may have a genetic code that would make it more likely for me to become an alcoholic. But just because I have a tendency toward alcohol abuse doesn't mean I can just give into that tendency and become an alcoholic. Genetic tendencies don't excuse behavior.

Review

You're in a science class when a fellow student tells the teacher he heard that homosexuality is genetic. What could you say to him and the class? How would you explain that homosexuality is not genetic? Record your thoughts below. Look back over the last few pages if you need some help.

_____

_____

_____

Message 2: Homosexuality Cannot Be Changed

The culture's second message, "homosexuality cannot be changed," is a logical conclusion if you believe homosexuality is genetic. If it's genetic, then you can't change it. You've probably heard this message, too. It sounds a lot like this:

"You can't change homosexuality. It's something you are, not just something you do."

"Homosexuality can't be changed. Psychiatrists say it's dangerous to try to change your sexuality."

"I can't change my sexual preference any more than I can change my height."

When evaluating this argument supporting homosexuality, it's important to remember what you learned earlier in this chapter: there is no scientific proof that homosexuality is genetic. While many studies have been conducted, none have given irrefutable evidence that homosexuality is based solely in a person's chromosomes.

How can you respond to the idea that homosexuality can't be changed? Simple. Find proof that the message is false. If homosexuals cannot change their behavior, then no homosexual would ever become a heterosexual because change is impossible.

The good news is that there is proof. People are being changed. Rather than reading a bunch of statistics about people who've experienced changed lives, read a couple of stories:

John grew up in a divorced home. His father was distant, and his mother was insecure. In high school he experienced his first homosexual encounter. His desire for love and acceptance from men led him to become a male escort, to dress like a woman, and to become an alcoholic. Through a strange series of events, John eventually left the homosexual lifestyle, went through in-depth counseling, and has experienced a changed life.

Anne was molested as a young child. As a result, to be a girl meant being vulnerable and being hurt, which she wouldn't allow herself to be. In college she joined a gay/lesbian group and eventually got involved in a lesbian relationship. Then, as God began to speak to her heart about her behavior, Anne began the slow process of turning away from homosexuality and experiencing healing and restoration.

John and Anne eventually met each other. They are now married and have two children. [18]

The stories of John and Anne Paulk are not isolated. In fact, many other people have experienced change. You can check out the Web sites in the appendix of this study to read about more stories of people being changed. The Bible even talks about changed lives. First Corinthians 6:9-11 says, "Do you not know that the unjust will not inherit God's kingdom? Do not be deceived: no sexually immoral people, idolaters, adulterers, male prostitutes, homosexuals, thieves, greedy people, drunkards, revilers, or swindlers will inherit God's kingdom. Some of you were like this; but you were washed, you were sanctified, you were justified in the name of the Lord Jesus Christ and by the Spirit of our God." Did you catch what Paul said? He listed off a bunch of different sins, including homosexuality, and told the church at Corinth that "some of you were like this." Notice the past tense. These people *were* idolaters. They *were* thieves and homosexuals. But now, Paul said, these people had been changed by Christ. What they had done in the past did not continue into the present. Change was possible. While repenting from homosexuality is very difficult, painful, and requires a great deal of work, people *can* be transformed.

Review
A teen in your youth group tells you that she's a lesbian. She say she thinks it's impossible for her to change because she's just "always been that way." What could you say to her? How would you explain that homosexuality can be changed? Record your thoughts below. Look back over the last few pages if you need some help.

_____

_____

_____

_____

Me//age 3: The 10 Percent Argument

You've probably heard people in the media talking about the large numbers of people who are homosexual. Since so many people are homosexual, it can't be wrong, can it?

In 1948, Alfred Kinsey, a researcher, published a study of the sexual behavior of over five thousand men. The study revealed that 37 percent of the men admitted to having one homosexual experience, and 10 percent claimed to have been homosexual for at least three years. Thus, the media and many scientists claimed that 10 percent of the population was homosexual.[19]

Problems with the 10 Percent Argument
1. Twenty-five percent of the men studied were prisoners—many of whom were sex offenders who may have been in prison for homosexual behavior.[20] (In the 1940s, when this study was con-

ducted, people could be arrested and imprisoned for homosexual behavior.) Since such a large number of men in the study were prisoners (where the likelihood of homosexual encounters increases sharply), the study did not accurately reflect the population at large.

2. Studies conducted since 1948 have disproven Kinsey's findings. For example, a 1993 survey of 3,321 American men indicated that only 2.3 percent of them had engaged in homosexual behavior in the last 10 years. Only 1.1 percent of men reported being exclusively homosexual. In 1989, a U.S. survey showed that no more than 6 percent of adults had any homosexual contacts, and only 1 percent of adults were exclusively homosexual.[21]

3. Just because 10 percent of the population does something doesn't make it right. What if 10 percent of the population were found guilty of murder? Would that make murder OK? Of course not. And more than 10 percent of the population probably commits adultery, but their behavior doesn't make adultery acceptable. So just because a group of people think it's OK to be a homosexual doesn't make it right.

Message 4: The Bible Doesn't Really Condemn Homosexuality

If you've listened to the news lately, you've probably heard a lot said about homosexuals, even in the church. In 2003, a man named Gene Robinson, openly homosexual, was ordained as a bishop in the Episcopalian church. He wrote that "ultimately, of course, Jesus Christ challenges us to take Him at His word, to accept the extravagance of His accepting love, to be the child of God we were created to be, no matter the cost—in order to better serve Him. I answered God's call to acknowledge myself as a gay man."[22] He, along with many other people, claims that God's Word doesn't condemn homosexuality. In fact, they would say, God affirms and celebrates their sexual identity as homosexuals.

What does God's Word really say about homosexuality? Does it contain clear commands against homosexuality? Or have those Scriptures been wrongly interpreted by *homophobics*, a word defined as *people who are afraid of homosexuals*, or hypocrites? Let's look in the next chapter to find out.

REFERENCES

[1]Dave Levinthal, "Package deal didn't turn out the way stowaway flier expected: Man winds up in jail after arriving in Dallas inside air cargo crate," *Dallas Morning News*, 9 September 2003, 1A.

[2] Barbara Mikkelson, "Tooth in Advertising," *Urban Legends Reference Pages* [online], 27 February 2001 [cited 3 February 2004]. Available from Internet: *www.snopes.com/cokelore/tooth.asp*.

[3]Ibid. "Rescuing Richard Nixon," *Urban Legends Reference Pages* [online], 16 October 1998 [cited 3 February 2004]. Available from Internet: *www.snopes.com/soons/legends.nixon.htm*.

[4]"Cigarson," *Urban Legends Reference Pages* [online], 10 July 2000 [cited 3 February 2004]. Available from Internet: *www.snopes.com/crime/clever/cigarson.asp*.

[5]"Crystal ball starts fire at Okla. home," *USA Today* [online], 29 January 2004 [cited 3 February 2004]. Available from Internet: *www.usatoday.com/news/offbeat/2004-01-29-flaming-orb_x.htm*.

[6]Barbara Mikkelson, "Drug Money," *Urban Legends Reference Pages* [online], 9 July 2002 [cited 3 February 2004]. Available from Internet: *www.snopes.com/business/money/cocaine.asp*.

[7]In that study, Hamer and his coworkers performed a "linkage study." In this kind of study, researchers identify a behavioral trait (such as homosexuality, violence, or alcoholism) that runs in a family. Then they look for a common DNA segment (or marker) on a particular chromosome. If the same segment is present consistently among family members who have the trait, then scientists propose that the gene causes the trait. For example, a scientist could study several generations of men in a family to determine if they all share a gene that makes them more prone to violence.

[8]Dean H. Hamer et al, "A Linkage Between DNA Markers on the X Chromosome and Male Sexual Orientation," *Science* 261 (July 1993): 321-27.

[9]George Rice, et al., "Male Homosexuality: Absence of Linkage to Microsatellite Markers at Xq28," *Science* 284 (April 1999): 665-667.

[10]Dean Hamer and Peter Copeland, *Living with Our Genes: Why They Matter More Than You Think* (New York: Bantam Doubleday Dell, 1998),188-89.

[11]Michael Bailey and Richard Pillard, "A Genetic Study of Male Sexual Orientation," *Archives of General Psychiatry* 48 (1991): 1089-96.

[12]David Gelman, "Born or Bred?" *Newsweek,* Vol. 119, Issue 8 (4 February 1992): 46.

[13]Simon LeVay, "A Difference in Hypothalamic Structure Between Heterosexual and Homosexual Men," *Science* 253 (August 1991): 1034-37.

[14]David Gelman, "Born or Bred?" 47.

[15]Joe Dallas, "Responding to Pro-Gay Theology, Part 1: Social Justice Arguments," *Exodus International, North America* [online], 1995-2001 [cited 4 December 2003]. Available from Internet: *www.exodus-international.org/library_church_21.shtml.*

[16]"Sexual Disorientation: Faulty Research in the Homosexual Debate," *Family* (A publication of the Family Research Council) (June 1992): 4.

[17]David Gelman, "Born or Bred?" 47.

[18]John and Anne Paulk, *Love Won Out* (Wheaton: Tyndale House Publishers, 1999).

[19]Alfred Kinsey et al., *Sexual Behavior in the Human Male* (Philadelphia: Saunders Press, 1948), 625.

[20]Judith Reisman, *Kinsey, Sex and Fraud: The Indoctrination of a People* (Layfayette: Huntington, 1990), 9.

[21]Joe Dallas, *A Strong Delusion* (Eugene: Harvest House Publishers, 1996): 126.

[22]Gene Robinson, "The Reverend Canon Gene Robinson Responds to Questions," *The Diocese of New Hampshire* [online], 11 November 2003 [cited 6 February 2004]. Available from Internet: *www.nhepiscopal.org/BishopSearch/The_Rev_Canon_V_Gene_Robinson.htm.*

Chapter 3 Notes

AN AUTHORITATIVE WORD
What Does the Bible Say About Homosexuality?

emember the third chapter of Genesis, in which the serpent deceived Eve? Do you remember the lie he fed Eve in the form of a question? He asked, "Did God REALLY say you must not eat from the tree. . . ?" In that moment, the serpent planted the seed of doubt in Eve's mind. She began to question what God had really said to her.

Sadly enough, Satan is still using that ploy to get people to question God's Word. "Is it really wrong to have sex if we both love each other?" "Is it really wrong to cheat on this test if everyone else is doing it?" "Is it really wrong to download this song illegally since the artists make so much money anyway?" And people have begun to ask, "Did God really condemn homosexuality in the Bible?" Many homosexuals will state that they believe in the Bible, but they think the Scriptures that speak negatively about homosexuality have been mistranslated (from the original language to English), misinterpreted (a wrong context applied to them), or misunderstood (what the writers were really trying to say). It is important to remember that, while the Bible talks about sex between a male and female as good and positive, there is no positive reference to homosexuality. No verse in the Bible says that homosexuality is good. What exactly does the Bible say about homosexuality? Let's take some time to find out.

The Levitical Law

One of the earliest references to homosexuality in the Bible is found in the Book of Leviticus. Before we discover what it says about homosexuality, let's take a look at the background of the book. If you've ever tried to read the whole Bible, you probably got bogged down in Leviticus. It's not light reading. At first glance it just seems like a bunch of rules and regulations that don't mean much to you and me living in the 21st century. It talks about how the Israelites (the people of God) were to offer their sacrifices to God; it outlined the food the Israelites were allowed to eat (pigs, rabbits, and owls were off limits, for example), and it explained the punishment for breaking God's commands. But why all the rules? Why were the people to offer sacrifices and limit what they ate or touched?

Because God is holy. He is completely different from you and me. He is unique, set apart, and utterly untouched by sin. Those who enter into a relationship with Him are called to be *holy*, which means "set apart and different," just as He is holy (Lev. 11:44). God wanted the Israelite people to be set apart—holy—as they entered into the tabernacle, the place where He actually dwelt among them. Not only were they to be set apart as holy for worship, but they were also to be set apart in their daily lives. Their lives were to be marked by an "otherness" or a difference compared with the sinful nations around them. When you're in a growing relationship with a holy God, your life will be different from those around you who don't know God.

Now that you know a little more about why Leviticus was written, take a few minutes to find out what it says about homosexuality.

The Prohibition and Punishment
Read Leviticus 18:22 and 20:13. Summarize both verses in the space provided.

_____
_____
_____
_____
_____
_____

In Leviticus 18:22 we find the command, "You are not to sleep with a man as with a woman; it is detestable." Later, Leviticus 20:13 specifies the punishment for breaking this command: "If a man sleeps with a man as with a woman, they have both committed an abomination. They must be put to death; their blood is on their own hands."

Unlike other laws that resulted in minor punishment, the command against homosexuality carried serious consequences—death. Other sins similar to this one were also punishable by death, including adultery (20:10); *bestiality*, which means "having sexual intercourse with an animal" (20:15), and incest (20:17-21).

Mistranslated, Misinterpreted, or Misunderstood?

Homosexuals deny that this Scripture condemns homosexuality. They argue that the Levitical law wasn't really condemning homosexuality and even if the passage did condemn homosexuality, that law doesn't apply to Christians anymore because believers live under grace, not the law. Let's look at their two arguments.

Dealing with Leviticus

First, let's deal with the law itself. According to some homosexuals, the word translated *detestable* (or abomination) in Leviticus 18:22 didn't really refer to homosexuality itself but instead referred to homosexuality connected with idol worship.[1] This word is used in the Bible several times to refer to the idol worship of surrounding nations, which clearly offended a holy God. Thus, in the opinion of homosexuals, when God said "it is detestable," He was only condemning homosexuality connected with pagan idolatry, not homosexuality between two loving, committed people.

There are two problems with this line of logic. First, the word *detestable* is used in other places in Scripture that do not refer to idol worship. Consider Proverbs 6:16-19, for example. It says that many things are detestable to God, including "arrogant eyes, a lying tongue, hands that shed innocent blood, a heart that plots wicked schemes, feet eager to run to evil, a lying witness who gives false testimony, and one who stirs up trouble among brothers." Idolatry is not mentioned in this passage, so the context of the word *detestable* is not limited only to idolatry.

The second problem with this line of logic is this: if these actions, such as homosexuality, listed in Leviticus 18 are prohibited only because of their connection with idolatry, then it would be OK to do those things as long as they don't involve idol worship.[2] In other words, incest, adultery, and bestiality are OK as long as you don't do those things in connection with worshiping an idol. Most people would never accept incest and adultery as OK. Scripture itself condemns these behaviors. (Check out Ex. 20:14 and Heb. 13:4.)

So we know this passage didn't apply just to idolatry. Clearly, God told the Israelites not to engage in homosexuality. Does that passage still apply to believers today? Homosexuals would say that they no longer live under the Old Testament law but instead live under grace.[3] According to this line of reasoning, you either hold to all of the Old Testament law or admit that the law no longer applies to Christians today.

How you would respond to someone who said that the Old Testament law against homosexuality didn't apply anymore? __

_____

_____

_____

Does It Still Apply?

Does the Old Testament law still apply to believers today? Well, it depends on what kind of law you're talking about—civil law or moral law. The laws in the Old Testament can be labeled one of two ways: (1) moral law or (2) civil or ceremonial laws. Moral laws included the Ten Commandments, while ceremonial laws included commands against touching a dead animal or eating a forbidden food. How can you tell whether a law was civil or moral? Mainly by the seriousness of the penalty attached to breaking that law. For example, committing adultery (Lev. 20:10), murder (Ex. 21:12), and rape (Deut. 22:25) all meant death. On the other hand, ceremonial laws involved a minor penalty (Ex. 22:4-5; Lev. 11:35, 17:15). Moral laws carried heavy consequences. Civil or ceremonial laws did not. Today, believers still follow God's moral law, such as not killing, committing adultery, and so forth.

How did Jesus treat the Old Testament laws? He understood the differences between the types of laws. He confronted the Pharisees for following ceremonial law while neglecting the "more important matters of the law—justice, mercy, and faith" (Matt. 23:23). He also set aside dietary laws—what a Jew could and could not eat (Mark 7:18-19). He clearly understood the difference between the types of laws. The ceremonial laws, like animal sacrifice for the payment of sins, were fulfilled in the sacrificial death of Jesus, and Christians have done away with these practices. However, moral laws still remain. And the command against homosexuality is one of those moral laws.

The Book of Roman/

Take a minute to look at a New Testament passage that talks about homosexuality. Read Romans 1:26-27 and summarize it in the space below:

_____

_____

_____

_____

The apostle Paul wrote the Book of Romans. His aim was to show that every person—male, female, Jew, Gentile (non-Jewish person)—is a sinner and can be forgiven only through Jesus' sacrificial death on the cross. In the first chapter of Romans, Paul explained that humanity's sinful condition results in God's wrath because a holy and righteous God cannot tolerate sin. In this chapter, he described what happens when the people God created stop worshiping their Creator and turn to sin. One of the symptoms of this sin problem is distorted sexuality—homosexuality. Other symptoms of this sin problem include murder, envy, gossip, and arrogance, which are also listed in this same chapter (Rom. 1:29-30).

Mi/tran/lated, Mi/interpreted, or Mi/under/tood?

In this passage, Paul said, "Their females exchanged natural sexual intercourse for what is unnatural. The males in the same way also left natural sexual intercourse with females" (v. 26-27). Homosexuals argue that these verses aren't talking about true homosexuals but rather heterosexuals who were trying to be unnaturally homosexual. In other words, the real sin is not homosexuality, but trying to do something that's contrary to a person's natural sexual tendencies. If a person was really a heterosexual and acted out in a homosexual manner, then that person sinned. If a true homosexual acted out his or her "natural" sexuality, then that person did not sin. In this viewpoint, Scripture condemns people for trying to change what comes naturally to them.

Pursuing the "Natural"

The heart of this line of logic is this: if something seems natural to you, then it's OK to pursue it. What's the problem? Our sinful nature is the problem. Human beings are sinful. We are born with a sinful nature. You don't have to teach a child to do wrong; you must teach a child to do right. Why? Because human beings are sinful at their very core. Because we have a sinful nature, what feels natural to us is sin. If every person pursued what was natural to him or her, then the other sins listed in Romans 1—murder, gossip, greed, deceit, and malice, just to name a few—would be acceptable if they felt natural. Just because something seems natural to you doesn't mean it's good!

In this passage, Paul used very specific words for our English words *men* and *women*. The Greek words Paul used for *men* and *women* are very specific in describing the gender of the person. Instead of saying, "People exchanged natural relations," Paul stated that men and women—two words that specifically refer to gender—acted outside of their natural functioning. Why are those two words so important? In using those specific words, Paul was referring to the biologically unnatural nature of homosexuality. Biologically, men are built to have a sexual relationship with women, not other men. Likewise, women are biologically structured to have sex with men, not women.[4]

One More Argument from Romans

Some homosexuals claim that these verses do not refer to homosexuality in general but instead refer to homosexuality expressed in the midst of idol worship. Again, nothing in the Scripture or the original language suggests that Paul was talking about idol worship. Even if homosexual acts were being done in connection with idol worship, Paul didn't declare homosexuality to be acceptable outside of idol worship. Paul didn't say, "Homosexuality is wrong if it's done in conjunction with idolatry, but it's OK if you're in a committed and loving relationship." Paul, writing under God's authority, didn't make any allowances for sinful behavior. Sin is always sin, even if it's said to be done in love.

A New Word Coined

Let's look at one more New Testament passage that talks about homosexuality.

Read 1 Corinthians 6:9-11.

What was Paul's point in these verses? _____
_____
_____

What specific sins are listed? _____
_____
_____

Does that mean these people cannot become believers? Why or why not? _____
_____
_____

What happened to the people Paul talked about? _____
_____
_____

In this passage Paul listed several sins, one of which was homosexuality. He wasn't saying that homosexuals (or people who are sexually immoral, adulterers, or male prostitutes) are forbidden to enter God's kingdom because they cannot be saved. Paul was simply pointing out that sinful people, apart from the forgiveness Christ offers, are condemned in their sin. He later said that some of those same people had been saved by Christ, repenting of their sinful lives and turning in obedience to Him.

Mistranslated, Misinterpreted, or Misunderstood?

Why is this passage important? Because it lists homosexuality as a sin. Many homosexuals claim that the word translated *homosexuals* in this passage doesn't really mean homosexual. In other words, it has been mistranslated. In their opinion it refers to male prostitution (which was common in Paul's day) or simply an immoral man. Paul was the first person to use this specific word for homosexuality, so according to the homosexual's argument, he wasn't really referring to homosexuality. If he had really wanted to condemn homosexual behavior, he would have used a word already in existence.

Not So Hard to Understand

It does seem a little curious that Paul created a new word to refer to homosexuality. But he coined at least 179 words in the New Testament,[5] words that had never been used before he created them. Therefore, since he used new terms all the time, this new word for homosexuality isn't too surprising. What is important is how Paul got this new word.

Time for another history lesson. When the Old Testament was written, it was written in Hebrew, the language of the Jewish people. Later, the Old Testament was translated into the Greek language so that Jews and others who didn't know Hebrew could understand the Scripture. This new translation was called the Septuagint. When Paul created the word *homosexual* in 1 Corinthians

6:9, he took part of his new word from the Septuagint. Guess which verses he used to create the new word? Leviticus 18:22 and Leviticus 20:13. Sound familiar? Those are the two Old Testament verses you looked at earlier—the ones that forbid homosexuality. What does this tell us? Paul wasn't talking about prostitution or just an immoral person. He was clearly talking about homosexuality. (By the way, the same word is also used in 1 Timothy 1:9-10, and the meaning is the same.)

One Laſt Argument

Some homosexuals would say that the biblical writers like Paul didn't understand homosexual attraction or behavior. And since they didn't have a concept of what homosexuality was all about, their writings about homosexuality don't really apply.

However, history tells us that homosexuality was prevalent in Paul's day. Plato and Aristotle both understood the concept and wrote about it. And being a Greek-educated man, Paul would have been aware of those teachings. In addition, a Jewish historian named Josephus, who lived around the same time as Paul did address the problem of homosexuality, so the biblical writers were familiar with it.[6]

Review Time

Let's review what we've learned about what Scripture says about homosexuality. Read each of the case studies. In the spaces provided, write a response to the scenarios. Look over the previous pages if you need help. Good luck!

Case Study 1

Jason comes to your Sunday school class on a regular basis. One day the class is discussing homosexuality. He says, "I know the Old Testament said homosexuality is wrong. But we don't really follow the Old Testament any more, so those laws don't apply anymore. I think homosexuality is OK."

_____

_____

_____

_____

Case Study 2

Samantha joins you at church one Sunday morning after a school party on Saturday night. During the sermon the pastor makes a passing comment about homosexuality. After the sermon, Samantha says, "I can't believe your pastor ripped on homosexuals like that. Doesn't he know that the writers back then didn't know anything about homosexuality? They wouldn't condemn it today."

_____

_____

_____

_____

Case Study 3

You're on a mission trip repairing a home in a low-income neighborhood. A guy approaches you, and he begins to talk to you. He says, "You know, you go to church, but the church shouldn't come down on homosexuals. The New Testament doesn't really preach against being gay. That writers were just telling people to do what comes naturally to them and to avoid prostitution."

_____
_____
_____
_____

Some Other Things People Might Say

While you may not be confronted with lots of questions about the specific Scriptures that talk about homosexuality, you'll probably face statements like the ones listed below. Under each one, list some possible responses you could give.

"Jesus never said anything about homosexuality."

_____
_____
_____
_____

"I'm a Christian, and I'm gay. How can that be true if homosexuality is wrong?"

_____
_____
_____
_____
_____

"Homosexuality is OK if both people truly love each other. It's wrong to deny someone love."

_____
_____
_____
_____

"I've tried to change, but I can't. God must have created me this way, so He wants me to be gay."

_____

_____

_____

_____

"A long time ago, the church misinterpreted the Bible to support slavery, and they were wrong. Now, the church is just misquoting the Bible to condemn homosexuals."

_____

_____

_____

_____

How did you do? Was it difficult to think of an answer? Here are some ways to respond to these arguments.

"Jesus never said anything about homosexuality."

It's true, Jesus never said anything about homosexuality. But just because Jesus didn't talk about a specific action doesn't make that action acceptable. Jesus never talked about incest or spousal abuse, but those actions are not acceptable. Other Scriptures talk about homosexuality, and those Scriptures are just as important as what Jesus said.

You and I really don't know if Jesus spoke about homosexuality. We just know the Gospel writers (Matthew, Mark, Luke, and John) didn't write it down if He did speak about it. (Check out John 21:25—Jesus did and said much more than what was written about Him!)

Although Jesus didn't say anything about homosexuality, He did affirm marriage. He talked about it in Mark 10:5-9, and He affirmed God's original intent of sexuality—between husband and wife.

"I'm a Christian and I'm gay. How can that be true if homosexuality is wrong?"

Just because you're a Christian doesn't mean you don't sin, and it doesn't mean that everything you do is OK in God's sight. Many people who are Christians cheat on their taxes. Some commit adultery. Lots of Christians overeat and don't take care of their bodies. Does that mean those actions are acceptable? No.

"Homosexuality is OK if both people truly love each other. It's wrong to deny someone love."

Love doesn't make sin OK. Two teenagers may love each other, but having sexual intercourse outside of marriage is still a sin. A married man may "fall in love" with another woman, but that "love" doesn't make adultery OK. God has placed boundaries on sexual relationships, and He doesn't offer an alternative plan for those who don't like His commands.

"I've tried to change, but I can't. God must have created me this way, so He wants me to be gay."

Every person struggles with sin. An alcoholic struggles with wanting to drink. A gossip struggles to keep his or her mouth shut instead of speaking unnecessarily. A person who cheats struggles to be honest. Just because a desire won't go away doesn't mean that desire is good or acceptable. In fact, Paul talked about his own struggle with sin (see Rom. 7:7-24). He called himself a wretched man because he struggled so much with sin. But he didn't say it was OK for him to give in to his sinful struggles because he was tired of fighting them.

"A long time ago the church misinterpreted the Bible to support slavery, and they were wrong. Now the church is just misquoting the Bible to condemn homosexuals."

It's true that some Christians misinterpret the Bible to make it agree with their own personal agenda. This doesn't affirm homosexuality. It just means people are human and make mistakes. The

Klu Klux Klan still uses Scripture to defend their racist, unbiblical actions. However, just because a person or a group of people misused Scripture in the past doesn't mean a person or a church is misinterpreting the Bible in the present, as in the case of homosexuality.

Keep this in mind: there's a big difference between calling a behavior sinful and persecuting the people who are involved in that sin. While slaves were treated horribly (beaten, denied the right to vote, treated like property, etc.) and the church was wrong to allow this practice, conservative Christians are not calling for the persecution of homosexuals. In fact, many believers want to reach out in love.[7]

REFERENCES

[1]Troy Perry, *Don't Be Afraid Anymore* (New York: St. Martin's Press, 1990), 341. As quoted in *A Strong Delusion* by Joe Dallas (Eugene: Harvest House Publishers, 1996), 192.

[2]Joe Dallas, *A Strong Delusion* (Eugene: Harvest House Publishers, 1996), 193.

[3]Mark Olson, "Untangling the Web," *The Other Side* 20 (April 1984): 25. As quoted in *Dark Obsession* by Timothy Dailey (Nashville: Broadman and Holman, 2003), 58.

[4]Joe Dallas, *A Strong Delusion*, 195.

[5]Ibid., 198.

[6]Timothy Dailey, *A Dark Obsession* (Nashville: Broadman and Holman, 2003), 62.

[7]Joe Dallas, *A Strong Delusion*, 175.

Chapter 4 Notes

BEING THERE
How Do I Help a Friend Who Is Struggling with Homosexuality?

You're playing basketball with a friend named John. Although he's normally the better player, you beat him soundly. It just doesn't seem like his head's in the game. Afterward, you comment on his being "on another planet." He looks at his feet, shuffles them back and forth, and after what seems like forever, he says, "I've been thinking about something lately, and I need to tell you. I think I'm gay."

63

You're hanging out with your friends at the mall when you notice Kelly walk in. Everybody knows that Kelly is a lesbian. Her girlfriend has even attended some of Kelly's volleyball games. Before you know it, the conversation centers on Kelly. Your friends start making fun of her, using derogatory terms such as *lesbo* and *dyke* as everyone laughs. There's even talk of following Kelly around the mall to see where she goes and what she does.

You're at youth camp one year, where students from different groups are placed into family groups for Bible study. On the second day, the group leader begins to discuss how we should accept people. He goes on to tell the group that the church should just follow Jesus' example and accept people as they are, including homosexuals. He says that Christians are supposed to love all people, regardless of their sexual preferences, so churches should not preach messages against people who choose a different lifestyle.

You're on a debate team. During one competition, homosexuality is one of the topics of discussion. The person you're debating explains that gays and lesbians should be afforded the same marital protection under the law as heterosexuals because the government has no place in deciding who should be allowed to marry. He claims that because homosexuality is hereditary, it should be protected under the law. He says that people who disagree are ignorant, biased, and intolerant because they refuse to affirm the homosexual lifestyle.

What would you do in each of these circumstances? Situations like these occur every day. As a Christian, you must be prepared for these instances when you face them (1 Pet. 3:15). Hopefully, this chapter will give you the tools to help you model Christ as you interact with people who are impacted by homosexuality.

What Jesus Taught

Who's your favorite teacher? What makes that teacher unique and special in your eyes? What did he or she do that was different from other teachers you've had? You have probably encountered a teacher who has impacted you in a memorable way. Maybe he kept your attention well. Perhaps she saw potential in you that no one else saw. Probably, he challenged you and encouraged you. And you learned from him or her.

In the space below, list your favorite teacher(s) and what made that teacher(s) special to you.

_____
_____
_____
_____
_____

People considered Jesus a great teacher. In fact, Scripture tells us that He taught with authority, unlike the teachers of the law in His day (Matt. 7:28-29). Crowds of people flocked to hear Him teach. On one occasion so many people crowded around to listen to Him at the seashore that He had to get into a boat and be rowed out to teach (Luke 5:1-3). His parables, stories, and illustrations made Scripture come alive. His teachings helped the people understand more clearly God's message of love and repentance.

In learning how to respond to people impacted by homosexuality, we can learn from the Great Teacher, Jesus. He told a story that can help us understand how best to treat those we encounter.

Read Luke 10:25-37.

This story contains several characters. In the space provided, record everything you learned about each person. Be sure to include what they said and did.

Expert in the law: _____
_____
_____

Jesus: _____
_____
_____

Man on the road: _____
_____
_____

The priest: _____
_____
_____

The Levite: _____
_____
_____

The Samaritan: _____
_____
_____

An expert in the law confronted Jesus to test Him. In the course of their conversation, the man asked an interesting question: "Who is my neighbor?" He wanted to know exactly who he had to love in order to fulfill the law. The man was expecting to trap Jesus, but instead Jesus gave him a lesson on loving people.

The man traveling from Jerusalem to Jericho was robbed, beaten, and left for dead. Along that same road to Jericho, a priest and Levite crossed the wounded man's path. Neither one stopped to help. Then along came a Samaritan, the hero in the story. While the term *Samaritan* may not mean anything to you and me, it got the attention of the crowd. Jews and Samaritans hated each other. Jews considered Samaritans as outsiders, unclean, and unlovely. Yet the only person to stop and care for the beaten man was a Samaritan. He bandaged the man's wounds, carried him to an inn, and paid for his stay. He used his own resources to care for a man he didn't even know.

Remember the expert's question to Jesus: who is my neighbor? Jesus didn't really answer the question. He didn't give the man a list of people to check off or a guideline to follow so he could feel better about how he treated others, especially those who were different than he was. Instead, Jesus challenged the expert in the law not to worry about who his neighbor was and to instead concentrate more on being a good neighbor to everyone.

Think about this story. How does it relate to our study of homosexuality? Record your thoughts below:

_____

_____

_____

_____

_____

Which of the characters from the story are you most like? Read a brief description of each and check the one that applies to you most:

_____ **The man who was beaten and robbed: treated horribly by someone; abandoned by everyone; in need of someone to love and care for him.**

_____ **The expert in the law: not really concerned about following Jesus; wasn't concerned about loving others; wanted to justify himself.**

_____ The priest or the Levite: didn't go out of his way or risk anything to help somebody; ignored the needs of others; wasn't willing to give to someone.

_____ The Samaritan: saw someone in need and helped the person; didn't care about labels, prejudice, or repayment; was willing to risk in order to help someone.

Take a few minutes to evaluate honestly your commitment to love people regardless of who they are or what they do. Then, in the space provided, record a prayer to God. Confess your prejudices and ask Him to help you be a neighbor to everyone who crosses your path. _____

_____

_____

_____

_____

What Jesus Did

When seeking to improve their skills, most athletes watch video footage of their sport. Sometimes they evaluate their own performance, perhaps by watching footage of a recent basketball game. Others don't watch films of themselves, but they study the great players in their sport instead. These students of the game will watch hours of film to learn how their heroes in the sport pivoted, swung, hit, threw, stood, tackled, blocked, kicked, and ran. Athletes know that when you want to learn from someone, you study the best example.

In discovering how to interact with people, we also need to learn from the best example. Scripture shows us that the best example is Jesus. Through His teaching, you've already been challenged to demonstrate love and compassion to the people around you, regardless of their status. Now learn from His example as you discover how Jesus Himself responded to different kinds of people.

Read Luke 5:27-32.

Pretend you are writing a news article for a newspaper. In the space below, write down the facts about the story: who was involved, what happened, the conflict, the reason for the conflict, and how Jesus responded to the conflict. Include the human element in your story—what the main characters were probably thinking and feeling. Use the following as a guide:

Who was involved: _____

_____

_____

What happened: _____

_____

_____

_____

The conflict: _____

_____

_____

_____

Reason for the conflict: _____

_____

_____

How Jesus responded: _____

_____

_____

What the "tax collectors and sinners" might have felt and thought: _____

_____

_____

What the Pharisees might have felt and thought: _____

_____

_____

_____

What Jesus might have felt and thought: _____

_____

_____

_____

If tabloid newspapers had existed in Jesus' days, this event would have probably made the front page with a headline like "Religious Leader Eats with Sinners" or "Rabbi Calls Sinners as Disciples." While Jesus' actions don't seem outrageous to you and me, they were scandalous to the people in His day. The religious leaders would never have spent time with tax collectors and sinners. They were outcasts because they didn't keep the law. Yet Jesus reached out to them. He challenged Levi (also called Matthew) to follow Him, that is, to be His disciple. No rabbi would ask a sinner, a tax collector, to be his student.

But the scandal didn't stop there. Not only did Jesus call Matthew to follow Him, but He also associated with Matthew's friends. When Matthew held a large banquet, Jesus engaged in more outlandish behavior by attending the feast and eating and drinking with these outcasts who didn't keep the law. In Jesus' day, eating a meal meant more than just passing the potatoes or sharing a dessert. Eating with a person implied that you accepted him or her and were willing to develop a relationship. Jesus was accepting "unacceptable" people in the Pharisees' eyes.

This ticked off the religious leaders. How could Jesus eat with such outcasts? They complained to Jesus' disciples about their Master's unorthodox behavior. The disciples didn't respond to their complaint, but Jesus did, and His answer was significant. He said,

"The healthy don't need a doctor, but the sick do. I have not come to call the righteous, but sinners to repentance" (Luke 5:31-32). He compared Himself to a doctor who wants to heal the sick. Although Jesus did heal people from physical problems, His main purpose was to heal people of the fatal spiritual sickness called sin. He knew the only way to cure sin was through a relationship with Him.

Verse 32 contains an important word: *repentance*. How would you define the word? Write your own definition in the space below:

_____

_____

_____

_____

The *Holman Bible Dictionary* provides information about *repentance*, defining it as "a feeling of regret, a changing of the mind, or a turning from sin to God . . . those who had made this commitment would demonstrate by their actions the change which they had made in their hearts . . . [it] entails both a rejection of sin and a positive response to God."[1] If you've ever watched a movie about the military, you've probably watched repentance in action. Soldiers march in one direction until commanded by their superior officer to "about face." At that point the soldiers stop, turn 180 degrees, and begin to march again in the opposite direction. That's the essence of repentance. It means "to turn away from sin and turn to God."

Why is this important? Because it shows that while Jesus loves and accepts sinners, He still calls people to turn away from their sin. Why? Because He is the doctor who wants to bring healing, and He knows that sin is a dreadful disease that destroys lives. He loves people too deeply to leave them in their sin and face the consequences.

Jesus' example provides us with the best role model for dealing with people. As His disciples, we are called to love others as He loved them—unconditionally. But as His followers, we must also call people to repentance, to turn away from the sin that will destroy their lives. Jesus didn't accept the sin of people; He called people away from it in a redemptive and loving manner. So should we.

Whether you are confronted by a gay activist who insists you agree with his viewpoint or find out that a good friend is battling with the temptation to follow her homosexual urges, keep in mind one central point: as a Christian, you are called to love people. James Dobson, founder of *Focus on the Family*, gives us something to think about:

> "Christians have a scriptural mandate to love and care for all the people of the world. Everyone is entitled to be treated with respect and dignity, even those who are living in immoral circumstances. There is no place for hatred, hurtful jokes, or other forms of rejection toward those who are homosexual. We cannot hope to win others to Jesus Christ if we insult and wound them. Remember, too, that Jesus was more compassionate toward the adulterous woman caught in the very act of intercourse— a capital offense in those days—than He was to hypocrites in the church."[2]

Practical Points

While it's true that love should guide your actions, you might have some questions, concerns, or uncertainties when it comes to the subject of homosexuality. You may not know how to respond to a friend or family member—what to say, what to avoid saying, things to remember. When talking with people about the subject of homosexuality, here are a few important principles to keep in mind.

1. Be aware of your emotions and feelings. What is your general attitude toward homosexuals? Are you afraid of them? Why? What prejudices do you have against people who are involved in homosexual behavior? Why? Sadly, many people, including Christians, treat homosexuals as if they were lepers to be avoided or ignored. Many are afraid that by hanging out with a homosexual, others will label them as a homosexual, too. Others even think they can get AIDS by spending time with a homosexual. Some think that being friends with a homosexual means you agree with that person's lifestyle.

The first step in overcoming fear and prejudice is to recognize those emotions and attitudes. Then you can work to build a bridge to reach out to people instead of a wall to keep people out.

Take a few minutes to write down how you feel about homosexuals. Are you afraid of them? Why? What prejudices do you have against them? Why? How would you react if a friend told you he or she was gay? Why do you think you'd respond that way? What questions would you have for him or her?

_____

_____

_____

_____

_____

2. Focus on the person, not on the behavior. Recognize that a homosexual is just like you in many ways. He or she has hopes, freckles, fears, dreams, hobbies, pet peeves, family, zits, intelligence, favorite foods, strengths, weaknesses, desires, and abilities. Don't let the label "homosexual" keep you from getting to know someone.

When I was in college, the school's cafeteria was divided down the middle by a salad bar. The athletes sat on one side of the cafeteria.

On the other side was my group of friends—the nerds. Each group stayed on its own side of the salad bar. Athletes didn't eat with nerds, and nerds didn't sit on the side of the room reserved for the jocks. It was as if an invisible barrier separated the two groups.

Then something odd happened. During the summer, one of the athletes wrote to me (back when you sent letters through the mail instead of the Internet!) while I was serving as a summer mission-ary. She was a Christian and just wanted to send a note of encour-agement to me while I was so far from home. When I got back from my mission experience, she and I began to do things together. We played on an intramural volleyball team together. We went to church together. Over time we became good friends. Why? Because one person was willing to go beyond the label to get to know me as a person. If she hadn't taken the first step, I would have missed out on a great friendship.

When you interact with people who are different from you, whether they are jocks, nerds, skaters, or involved with homo-sexuality, take the risk to get to know the person as a unique and valuable individual instead of just labeling him or her. When you build relationships, you open the door that allows you to share your faith. When others get to know you as a person, they will be more willing to hear about your relationship with Christ.

3. Remember that Scripture condemns homosexual behavior, not homosexual people. Many individuals have protested the homosexual lifestyle by waving banners and picket signs embla-zoned with such slogans as "God hates fags." God does not hate homosexuals. He loves them; He died for them. But He does hate the sin of homosexuality. He hates all sin, including cheating, lust, and gossip. He desires people to live in unbroken union and fel-lowship with Him. Sin, no matter what kind it is, places a wedge between God and His people.

Think about it like this: You and your parents have a close relationship. One day, though, you take the car without permission, go drinking with your friends, and wreck the car, wrapping it around a telephone pole. When your parents arrive at the scene of the accident, they are visibly upset. They are angry and hurt. When you disobeyed them, you hindered your relationship with them, damaging the trust and honor built between parent and teen. You wrecked the car. You put people in danger. You could lose your license. While they love you unconditionally, they are unhappy at your behavior.

Get the connection? God loves you unconditionally, but when you disobey His commands set forth in His Word, He doesn't like your rebellion against Him. He loves you but hates the sin.

4. Remember to dialogue, not argue. What's the difference? To dialogue with someone means listening to another person's beliefs even if you strongly disagree with those beliefs. When you dialogue, you ask questions to understand more; you express your own beliefs calmly and clearly; you allow the other person the right to believe something you don't. In your dialogue is a tone of respect for the other person. Arguing, on the other hand, means trying to force the other person to agree with you. In arguing, your goal is not to learn from each other or to exchange ideas. The goal is to win. Arguments are often just fights in which both people leave hurt and frustrated.

5. Sometimes you'll need to agree to disagree. When you're talking with someone who is convinced that homosexuality is a valid and biblical lifestyle, you may just have to agree to disagree. Arguing with that person will probably accomplish little except to drive a wedge between the two of you. Keep in mind that acknowledging another viewpoint isn't the same as agreeing with it. Agreement means acceptance. For example, you can acknowledge that your best friend thinks it's OK to cheat in school because it doesn't really hurt anyone. However, you don't have to agree with your best friend that cheating is OK. You have the right to disagree respectfully. You don't have to agree on everything in order to be friends.

6. Watch your language. Do you like being called fat? What if someone called your best friend ugly? How do you feel when classmates gossip about you? Nobody likes to be the object of harmful words or rumors, including people who struggle with their sexual identity. When you're with your friends, avoid jokes that poke fun at homosexuals. Don't use harmful names or labels. Don't start rumors about girls who act masculine or guys who act feminine. Proverbs 10:19 says, "When there are many words, sin is unavoidable, but the one who controls his lips is wise." Remember: words can leave deep scars inside. Be wise and hold your tongue.

7. Remember not to be a gossip. When a person shares with you struggles about his or her sexual identity, don't blab that information to everyone you know. It's not meant to be shared with your best friend, your parents, or a buddy on the Internet. Proverbs 16:28b states that a gossip separates close friends. In other words, you won't keep close friends for long if you don't keep your mouth shut. If a friend or family member shares that he or she is struggling with homosexuality, that person has shared something very deep and intimate. It is not meant to be broadcast across your school or church. You can encourage a friend to share with an adult who can provide counsel and godly information, but it's not your job to share such information to everyone. There's one exception to this rule: Sometimes teenagers who struggle with homosexuality harm themselves (cutting, suicide attempts, and so forth) in order to deal with the overwhelming emotions. If a friend threatens to harm himself or others, tell a trusted adult. He or she can get your friend some help. In that situation, your friend might get mad at you, but sometimes friends must do what's best for a friend, not necessarily what a friend wants.

8. Be real. Think about it: Do you want to spend time with people who pretend their lives are perfect? Are you drawn to role models who don't struggle with sin? Are you more inclined to listen to someone who has it all together or someone who struggles in life just like you but clings to Jesus as his or her Hope? If you're like most teenagers, you want to learn from and hear from people who are walking the same journey of faith—complete with its struggles, battles, frustrations, and failures. You probably admire people who work through a trial and are stronger in their faith because of it.

If you desire honesty, integrity, and transparency, don't you think other people desire the same character traits in you? When you talk with friends or family members who are struggling with an issue, whether it be homosexuality, premarital sex, or drinking, honestly admit that you face temptation, too, and that you're not immune to the lure of sin. Let them know that you depend on God's strength to help you through those weak times (2 Cor. 12:9-10).

9. Don't focus on homosexuality as the only topic of your conversations. In the movie *Finding Nemo*, a fish named Dori has short-term memory loss. At one point in the movie, however, she remembers an important name and address. She's so excited about actually remembering something (remember, she can't remember!) that she repeats the same name and address over and over and over and over again until she completely irritates her traveling companion Marlin (Nemo's father). It was the only thing she said for a while, and it got on Marlin's nerves.

When you have a friend who's talking about his or her struggle with homosexuality, keep in mind that he or she might not want to talk about it all the time. Like Marlin, your friend may get irritated or turned off if this struggle is the only topic of your conversation. Be willing to talk about other things that are common bonds or interests—school, family, favorite bands, sports, and so forth.

On the other hand, don't avoid the subject if it comes up. Don't try to change the topic of conversation to more comfortable ground. If your friend wants to talk, be willing to listen. Don't be afraid of the topic. And don't worry about having all the answers. Most friends just want someone who will listen to them.

10. Give honest feedback. If a friend shares with you that he or she is contemplating a homosexual lifestyle, you may have mixed feelings, confusing thoughts, and lots of questions. That's OK. Honestly and respectfully share your thoughts, feelings, and questions. You can say things like, "I need some time to think about it, OK? But don't worry. We're still friends, and I still care about you as a friend." You might want to ask questions to understand more, such as "How long have you been feeling this way?" "Has something happened to lead you to this decision?" "Have you shared your thoughts and feelings with anyone else?" "Can you help me understand what you're thinking and feeling? I've never dealt with this issue before, but I want to understand what you're going through."

Putting It all Together

Below are the case studies you read at the beginning of this chapter. Read them again. Based on what you've learned in this chapter, write down some ways you could deal with each situation.

You're playing basketball with a friend named John. Although he's normally the better player, you beat him soundly. It just doesn't seem like his head's in the game. Afterward, you comment on his being "on another planet." He looks at his feet, shuffles them back and forth, and after what seems like forever, he says "I've been thinking about something lately, and I need to tell you. I think I'm gay."

_____

_____

_____

_____

_____

_____

You're hanging out with your friends at the mall when you notice Kelly walk in. Everybody knows that Kelly is a lesbian. Her girlfriend has even attended some of Kelly's volleyball games. Before you know it, the conversation centers around Kelly. Your friends start making fun of her, using terms such as lesbo and dyke as everyone laughs. There's even talk of following Kelly around the mall to see where she goes and what she does.

_____

_____

_____

_____

_____

_____

_____

You're at youth camp one year, where students from different groups are placed into family groups for Bible study. On the second day the group leader begins to discuss how we should accept people. He goes on to tell the group that the church should just follow Jesus' example and accept people as they are, including homosexuals. He says Christians are supposed to love all people, regardless of their sexual preferences, so churches should not preach messages against people who choose a different lifestyle.

_____

_____

_____

_____

_____

_____

You're on a debate team. During one meet, homosexuality is one of the topics of discussion. The person you're debating explains that gays and lesbians should be afforded the same marital protection under the law as heterosexuals because the government has no place in deciding who should be allowed to marry. He claims that because homosexuality is hereditary, it should be protected under the law. He says that people who disagree are ignorant, biased, and intolerant because they refuse to affirm the homosexual lifestyle.

_____

_____

_____

_____

_____

_____

_____

_____

What personal situation have you faced? What case study could you write based on your own experience? Use the space below to write down experiences you've had like the case studies you've read. How can you deal with these now that you've learned more about how to respond in a Christlike manner?

_____
_____
_____
_____
_____
_____
_____
_____
_____

P.S. Some Things Not to Say

In this chapter, you've learned that Jesus is your role model for treating people with respect and love. While Jesus didn't approve of others' behavior, He did reach out to them in mercy and compassion. You've discovered how to relate to others when talking about homosexuality.

One last note: try to avoid some of the following hurtful statements. Consider it the "Top 10 Worst Things to Say to a Friend Who's Struggling with Homosexuality.'

1. You can't be serious! You? Gay? Yeah, right!
2. You'll get over it. It's just a phase. Remember when you wanted to be a truck driver?
3. You're going to hell. It's the unforgivable sin.
4. Man, is your mom gonna flip! And your dad! He's gonna kill you!
5. If you just pray about it, it'll go away.

6. You're not gay. You just haven't met the right person yet; let me introduce you to . . .
7. Don't tell anyone else. I don't want anybody knowing I'm friend with a homosexual.
8. Wait 'til I tell the guys on the football team!
9. You're not attracted to me, are you?
10. I thought you were better than that.

References

[1] Trent C. Butler, Gen. Ed., *Holman Bible Dictionary* (Nashville: Holman Bible Publishers, 1991), 1175-76.

[2] James Dobson, *Complete Marriage and Family Home Reference Guide* (Carol Stream: Tyndale House Publishers, Inc., 2000): 404-05.

Chapter 5 Notes

Chapter 5 Notes

A SOLID FOUNDATION
How Do I Develop Healthy Relationships With Others?

If you had lived near Mount St. Helens in 1980, you would have known the importance of paying attention to warning signs. On May 18, 1980, around 8:32 a.m., this volcano erupted violently. About 1.8 cubic miles of the mountain avalanched down at 150 miles per hour. A 180-300 mph blast of hot gases and rock covered 360 square miles in a matter of minutes. A huge column of gas and ash rose 15 miles in 15 minutes. The ash from the mountain reached neighboring Spokane, over 250 miles away, in just 3 1/2 hours. Fifty-seven people were killed. The mountain lost a quarter of a mile in height. The damage from the volcanic blast reached a staggering one billion dollars.

The mountain didn't erupt without warning. As early as March 20, volcanologists (that's people who study volcanoes, not a species from *Star Trek*) studying Mount St. Helens noted changes within the mountain. They studied rises in magma levels and an increase in sulfuric gases. On March 27, the mountain spewed a minor eruption and created a crater on the summit, a sign that a much larger eruption loomed ahead. Scientists measured an increased risk of a landslide and a bulge on the mountain. They noted earthquakes under the volcano. And after three fairly calm days of little activity, the mountain erupted in a mass of fury.[1]

During those three quiet days, people began to think that it was safe to go back onto the mountain, back into their homes. However, officials and scientists were hesitant to allow folks back into the danger zone for one simple reason: they saw the warning signs. Something dangerous was fast approaching.

Signs are important. Whether warning signs of an impending volcanic eruption or the positive signs that a tree is producing fruit, signs give us clues. They help us to know about impending danger (like a tornado) or upcoming joy (like the birth of a child). Signs also help us know whether a relationship is healthy or unhealthy.

When discussing homosexuality, it's important to talk about healthy relationships. Many homosexual relationships develop because the people in the relationship don't know how to develop healthy friendships. Many times the friendship starts out healthy but gets off track and develops into a homosexual relationship. In this chapter, you'll explore signs—characteristics—of a healthy relationship.

Friendship in the Bible

God's Word specifies some characteristics that should be evident in any healthy relationship with the same or opposite sex. See the chart on page 88. Read each of the Scriptures. For each one, write down the characteristic of a good friend. Next to that characteristic, provide an illustration of that characteristic in action. An example is provided for you.

Hopefully, you discovered the following characteristics about friendships:

1. Friends forgive each other (Prov. 10:12). Friends don't hold grudges and don't stir up trouble to get even with someone. Friends allow others to make mistakes and recognize that nobody is perfect. Everyone will let you down at some point. In a healthy relationship, you don't use guilt over past failures to get what you want. (For example, "Don't forget to call me before you leave for the mall. Remember what you did last time? You forgot to call me, and I was left at home alone.") That's not friendship. That's manipulation.

Who is someone you need to forgive? Why is it difficult to forgive that person? Against whom are you holding a grudge?

_____

_____

_____

_____

_____

2. Friends take time to learn about each other (Prov. 12:26). Good friendships are developed slowly, not quickly or intensely. When you're building a solid friendship, you build it over a long period of time. You allow roots to grow—roots of shared experiences, common interests, and trust and respect. Over time you learn to trust each other and share more deeply. However, if your relationship

SCRIPTURE	CHARACTERISTICS OF A GOOD FRIEND	EXAMPLE
Prov. 10:12	*Developed slowly over time, not quickly and intensely*	*Take time to know each other; don't share secrets too soon.*
Prov. 12:26		
Prov. 16:28		
Prov. 17:17		
Prov. 18:24		
Prov. 27:17		
Eccl. 4:9-10		
John 15:12-13		

developed quickly without a solid foundation, there's a good chance it won't last—it may not be healthy. There's no shortcut to healthy, solid friendships. They just take time.

Think about your deepest friendship. What shared experiences do you have? What are your common interests? How have you developed trust over time? _____

_____

_____

_____

3. Friends don't gossip—even when they're mad at each other (Prov. 16:28). How often have you been guilty of this? A friend hurts you or makes you mad, so you don't talk to him or her. Instead, you call another friend and talk about the person who hurt or angered you. This verse says that gossip separates friends. You can't develop a good friendship without trust; gossip kills trust.

Apply the simple formula below before talking about someone or something. If what you want to say doesn't pass the tests, then keep your comments to yourself.2

T–Is it true?
H–Is it helpful?
I–Is it inspiring?
N–Is it necessary?
K–Is it kind?

Have you ever been the victim of gossip? How did you feel? Do you gossip now even though you know how badly it can wound someone? Why or why not? _____

_____

_____

_____

_____

4. Friends stick with you through the rough times (Prov. 17:17; 18:24). Good friends hang in there with you through the worst times in your life, whether it's your parents' divorce, bad grades, the death of a family member, or a traumatic breakup. In their book, *Best Friends,* George and Karen Grant write, "There is no greater solace in times of trouble than the concern of a friend. Somehow they can comfort us . . . often even without words. They know us. They understand us. They care for us. All too often the great men and women through the ages were able to achieve what they did only because they had the recourse of friendship in times of adversity."[3]

Who has helped you through a rough time? What was the situation? How did your friend help you? _____

_____

_____

_____

_____

What would you do if a friend were struggling with homosexuality? Would you still be friends with that person? Why or why not? What does your answer reveal about your friendship? __

_____

_____

_____

5. Friends sharpen each other's character (Prov. 27:17). A friend will tell you when you're wrong and won't let you make a stupid mistake. A friend will challenge you to think outside the box, to take risks, to try something new, to see things from a different perspective. In a loving way, a friend will affirm your strengths and point out your weaknesses. A friend is willing to make the hard calls: "You really don't need to be dating that person. He (she) is bad news." "Steroids will mess up your body. You don't need to be using them." "Homosexuality won't provide what you're looking for."

"Moving in with your dad is a bad idea. You're just mad at your mom because she enforces rules, and you know your dad won't." Having a friend who sharpens you makes you a better person.

Who has sharpened you recently? Did you appreciate that person's honesty? How have you sharpened a friend? _____

_____

_____

_____

6. Friends help carry the burden in hard times (Eccles. 4:9-10).
When I got married, I moved my belongings from an apartment to my husband's home. Only I didn't have to move everything by myself. A group of friends from my church showed up on a rainy Saturday morning, and we moved everything together. Why did my friends help? Was it because I offered pizza after the work was done? They could have ordered pizza and stayed indoors. Was I paying them? Get real. They helped because that's what friends do—they carry the burden when necessary. Because of their help, we accomplished in two hours what would have taken days. In fact, without the help of strong guys, my entertainment center would still be sitting in the corner of the living room in that apartment. The eight-foot bookshelf would be a permanent fixture. I just couldn't have done it alone.

The same holds true with burdens in our lives. True friends will help carry the burden of a divorce, a death, or just a miserable day. When a friend helps you, the pain doesn't go away, but it's more bearable. And you don't feel so alone in the midst of the struggle.

When has someone carried a burden with you? What was the burden? How did you feel knowing you weren't alone? _____

_____

_____

_____

7. Friends are willing to sacrifice (John 15:12-13). There's a story about two soldiers in Wold War II that illustrates this point. The pair enlisted together, went through basic training together, and were shipped overseas together. They fought side by side. One night during an attack, one of the men was critically wounded and was unable to get back to the foxhole. His friend in the foxhole tried to rescue him, but an officer pulled him back in, knowing it was suicidal to try to rescue the man.

However, when the officer turned his back, the man in the foxhole darted out in the midst of the firefight in order to rescue his friend. In a few minutes the man returned. He was wounded, and his friend was dead. The officer yelled at him, "What a waste! He's dead, and you're dying. It wasn't worth it."

The man replied, "Oh, yes it was. When I got to him, the only thing he said was, 'I knew you'd come, Jim.'"[4]

True friendship is sacrificial. You may never be in a world war with a friend, but you will be faced with situations in which you must choose between selfishness and sacrifice. Will you donate bone marrow for a friend's brother? Will you tutor a friend instead of heading to the mall? Will you give up your summer vacation to help a friend repair his house after a flood? Will you sacrifice your personal comfort to share Christ with a friend who is destined to hell because he doesn't know how to be saved?

Who has demonstrated sacrificial friendship toward you? How have you sacrificed for a friend? _____
_____

8. Other: What other characteristics are indicators of a good friendship? List them below. Also list why those characteristics are important. _____
_____
_____

Take some time to evaluate your friendships. See the chart on page 94. In the space provided, list several of your closest friends and significant others (boyfriends/girlfriends). Rate your relationship (A+ is great, F is really bad) based on the characteristics you've discovered today. Be honest! Note that the far right column is empty. In that column, list one other characteristic that you think is most crucial in a healthy relationship.

Other Signs of a Healthy Friendship

No friendship is perfect because friendships are made up of two people, and people aren't perfect. But just as a basketball player seeks to improve his or her skills on the court or an artist takes a class to learn more about his or her craft, you can strive to develop healthy relationships. Check to see if your friendships involve:

Fun. Friends spend time doing things they enjoy. They go to movies, wash out the gutters, play ball, listen to music, work on cars, paint a house, drive, play on the computer, watch TV, study together, go to a dance recital, wash a car . . . you get the idea. While no friendship is fun all the time, friends generally like being together. If your only common interest and source of recreation is fighting, you probably need to evaluate whether the friendship is worth keeping.

Freedom. Friends don't control each other or demand loyalty. They allow each other the freedom to have other friends, to spend time apart, and to grow independent of each other. If you get jealous because your friend talks to someone else or spends quality time with someone other than you, you're treading on thin ice. Take a step back and allow your friend some freedom. Don't try to control him or her.

Inclusive of others.[5] Healthy friends are not self-absorbed or consumed by each other. They don't seclude themselves and refuse to engage with other people. Good friends don't have to spend

Name of Friend	Forgiving	Built Over Time	Don't Gossip	Stick With You	Sharpen You	Carry the Burden	Sacrificial

all their time together "evaluating the relationship." They enjoy spending time in groups and always allow for new people to join in. In solid friendships, there's always room for more.

Appropriate physical touch. Good friendships maintain solid boundaries. Stay away from actions that are reserved for marriage relationships. Even be careful about hugs. A prolonged hug can trigger a sexual response. Actions reserved for marriage are definitely off-limits, including touching genital areas, sexual intercourse, and so forth. Once you cross these boundaries, especially those explicitly sexual in nature, the friendship is in serious trouble. Those boundaries protect a friendship.

Healthy emotional attachment. Friends "are not mentally or emotionally preoccupied. . . . We do not fantasize about him or her. It's not that we don't think about our friends or care deeply for them—they just don't hold any magnetic power over out thought life or emotions."[6] If all your spare time, all your spare energy, and all your spare money are spent on one other person, the relationship isn't healthy.

Signs of an Unhealthy Relationship
You've discovered what God's Word says about friendship, and you've evaluated your relationships. You've even looked at some general characteristics that should be present in your friendships. Now, spend a few minutes thinking about some signs of unhealthy relationships.

In the space provided below, list things that might be evidence of an unhealthy relationship: _____
_____
_____
_____
_____
_____

Just like volcanologists look for warning signs of impending danger, you can also look out for warning signs of an unhealthy relationship.

Destruction of property or person. Throwing objects at someone when you're mad is inappropriate. Hitting or slapping someone is abusive. Threatening is wrong. (I'll tell everyone about _____ if you don't do what I want.) If this characterizes your relationship, get out before you or someone else gets hurt. Then get some help.

Blame. When you use blame, you try to shift responsibility to someone else. Blame sounds like this: I only did that because you_____ (fill in the blank). Remember, you are responsible for your own behavior. No one makes you do anything. You have a choice in how you will respond.

Intense jealousy. This level of jealousy may be demonstrated by "checking up" on the person's activities, calling repeatedly to make sure the other person doesn't go anywhere without you, driving by the person's home, or reading his or her email from other friends to make sure you're not left out.

Emotional abuse. Emotional abuse can take many forms: putting someone down, playing mind games, harassment, intimidation, the silent treatment, using derogatory names, threatening to kill yourself, and humiliation. These are signs of a seriously unhealthy relationship.

Separation anxiety. When small children leave a parent, they often experience separation anxiety. They don't want to be alone. In an unhealthy relationship, one or both friends cannot be apart. They cannot make decisions without first consulting the other person. They cannot live without the other person and think they can't make it on their own.

Case studies

Now that you've examined some characteristics of healthy and and unhealthy friendships, put your mind to the test. For each of the case studies, determine whether the relationship is healthy. Then explain why.

Case Study 1: John called Cindy to see if she wanted to go to the movies, but she said that she wasn't feeling well and was going to stay home. About an hour later, John jumped in his truck and drove over to her house to see if her car was there. It wasn't. John was furious and vowed to get her back for lying to him.

Healthy or not? Why? _____

_____

_____

_____

Case Study 2: Jamie and Kelly have been friends since they were in kindergarten. They go to the same school, play on the same basketball team, and attend the same church. However, they both enjoy being with other people. Days may go by before they talk to each other again, but when they do, they just pick up where they left off.

Healthy or not? Why? _____

_____

_____

_____

Case Study 3: Beth's father died six months ago. Her friend Paula listened and cared for Beth through the whole ordeal. Paula really enjoyed having someone to take care of. However, Beth seems to spend all her time with Paula now. She is afraid Paula will leave her. Paula likes the attention Beth gives her and is afraid Beth will do something stupid without her.

Healthy or not? Why? _____

_____

_____

_____

Case Study 4: John and Jeff have been best friends for years. They're both committed Christians and leaders in the youth group. When Jeff's parents divorced, though, things changed. Jeff began to withdraw from everything—church, basketball, and even his friendship with John. After a few months, John confronted Jeff and challenged him to get back into church and to start spending time with friends again.

Healthy or not? Why? _____

_____

_____

_____

Write Your Own Story

Now that you've read case studies and determined which ones were healthy relationships, take time to write about your own friendships.

In the space below, write about your strongest friendship. What characteristics make this friendship healthy? What do you enjoy about the other person? Why is this friendship valuable to you? If you can't think of any healthy friendships, write about a friendship on which you'd like to work.

_____

_____

_____

_____

An Example to Live By

You've learned a lot about friendship in this chapter. You've learned to recognize the strengths and weakness in your relationships. You've also learned how to spot the warning signs for dangerous friendships. You've examined your own friendships to see where they need work. And you've taken steps to make sure your friendships are healthy. Let the following story be a reminder of what friendship is all about.

The Men's Room is a hair salon in California. It's a remarkable place, not because of the chairs, the decor, the location, or even the stylists. It's important because of what took place there: 13 fifth-grade boys lined up there to get their heads shaved. Why? Because they cared about a friend.

Their classmate Ian O'Gorman, 11 years old, was about to undergo chemotherapy for lymphoma, and he was sure to lose his hair. Rather than lose it in clumps, Ian decided to shave it instead. To his surprise, his friends wanted to join him. The students didn't want their friend to stick out or to feel awkward. Kyle Hanslik, one of the "Bald Eagles" (as the boys now call themselves), talked to the other boys, and then one of their parents started a list. They all went to the barber shop together and all came back bald. The boys' teacher, Jim Alter, was so inspired that he also shaved his head. They plan on sticking with their friend. "When Ian gets his next CAT scan, if they decide to do more chemotherapy, we'll shave our heads for another nine weeks," said Erik Holzhauer, one of the Bald Eagles.[7]

Wrapping It Up

Remember, many homosexual relationships develop because one or both of the people don't know how to develop healthy friendships. While the relationship may start out healthy, it gets off track. By developing the principles for healthy friendships that you've learned about in this chapter, and by knowing the warning signs of unhealthy relationships, you can develop friendships that honor God and bring the fulfillment He designed.

Final Thoughts

In this book, you've learned and digested lots of information about homosexuality. You discovered God's design for human sexuality—between male and female within the context of marriage. When sin entered the picture, people abandoned God's plan for them in pursuit of their own plan. You also learned that while homosexuality is a sin, it is no better or no worse than any other sin. We're all equal at the foot of the cross—equally needing His love and forgiveness. You've also learned that what culture spouts as "scientific proof" that homosexuality is genetic isn't quite so cut and dried. You've learned to think critically about messages our culture is sending about homosexuality, and you've learned what God's Word says about it. In the latter chapters, you discovered how to help friends who are struggling or who have questions about homosexuality. You've also learned how to develop healthy relationships with others and how to spot the warning signs that a friendship may be headed in a negative direction.

You may still have questions about homosexuality. That's OK. Talk with a youth minister, pastor, or parent. While they may not know all the answers, they will be willing to work with you to find them. Some of your questions may be contained in the next section of this book, "Questions Teenagers Ask." If you don't have any questions, reading this section may help you as you encounter others who have questions. Also, you might want to check out the section "Additional Resources." It contains books, Web sites, and organizations whose specialty is helping people address this issue.

Homosexuality is a tough issue to tackle. With God's help, you can navigate the questions and feelings you're dealing with. And don't forget this: No matter what your struggle, whether it be homosexuality or steroids, remember that God loves you. Nothing you do (or don't do) will change His deep love for you. He wants the best for your life because He loves you.

REFERENCES

[1] John Seach, "Mount St. Helens Volcano," Volcano Live [online], cited 29 January 2004. Available from Internet: *www.volcanolive.com/sthelens2.html.*

[2] Alan Redpath, "Gossip," Sermonillustrations.com [online], cited 30 January 2004. Available from the Internet: *www.christianglobe.com/Illustrations/theDetails.asp?/whichOne=g&whichFile= gossip.*

[3] George and Karen Grant, *Best Friends* (Nashville: Cumberland House Publishing, Inc., 1998), 17.

[4] Alan Carr, "Elijah: Prophet of Courage and Confrontation," *The Sermon Notebook* [online], 2003 [cited 30 Jan 2004]. Available from Internet: *www.sermonnotebook.org/elijah/1%20kings%2019_15-21.htm.*

[5] Bob Davies and Lori Rentzel, *Coming out of Homosexuality* (Downers Grove, Ill.: InterVarsity Press, 1993):119.

[6] Ibid., 119.

[7] "Kindest Cut," *People Magazine*, Vol. 41 Issue 13 (1994): 60.

Chapter 6 Notes

APPENDIX 1: Questions Teenagers Ask

Question 1: I was in the locker room and looked at the others while we were changing clothes. Does that mean I'm a homosexual?

Answer: A good question to ask yourself is this: Why were you looking at the others in the locker room? The teenage years can be very confusing, especially with all the changes you're experiencing physically. Guys, you'll go through a growth spurt, produce pubic hair, facial hair, chest hair, and armpit hair. Your larynx will grow, causing the voice to change. Your shoulders will widen, your muscles will get thicker, and you'll sweat more. Your penis and scrotum will also grow. Girls, you'll also experience a growth spurt, and you'll produce pubic hair. You'll begin menstruation, or "get your period." Your breasts will begin to develop.

For you to look at others in the locker room to compare yourself is natural. It does not mean you're a homosexual. You're just wondering how you "measure up" to others your age. Are they experiencing the same changes you've faced? Are your breasts the same size? Do others have as much pubic hair as you? These are common questions teenagers ask themselves.

When you begin to compare yourself to others, keep in mind that you're a unique person, so you may not grow and change at the same pace as others. Just be patient. Changes will come in time. But remember, you may never be as tall as someone else. You may never develop chest hair. You may have smaller breasts than others. That's OK. God created you uniquely. Don't listen to the lies of the media that tell you you're inferior if you don't have a six-pack of abs or a pencil-thin waist. Being a real man or real woman is not about physical perfection. It's about being a well-rounded person, emotionally, physically, and spiritually.

Question 2: I'm attracted to someone of my same gender. Does that mean I'm a homosexual?

Answer: Let me ask you a question in return: what attracts you to this person? Does this guy or girl pay attention to you? Does he or she make you feel important? Loved? Valuable? Everybody wants to be loved; everyone wants to know that they're important. And everyone—whether they're 13 or 83—wants to know that they're valuable. Naturally, you'll be drawn to people who make you feel good about yourself. That's normal. It doesn't mean you're a homosexual. Keep in mind, though, that another person cannot meet all your needs. Don't put another person on a pedestal. Don't think you can't survive without him or her or that no one else will love or accept you. Your self-esteem must be based on God's love for you, not on another person. People will disappoint you, but God is always faithful.

Maybe you want to be around this person because he or she is popular. Perhaps that person exhibits qualities you admire and want to develop—leadership, compassion, wisdom, and so forth. It's natural to be drawn to those kinds of people. You can learn from others. Keep in mind, though, that God created you uniquely and wonderfully. While you may never be the most popular guy or girl at school, you are important. It doesn't matter if you become the captain of the football team or the president of the debate club. You have a unique place in God's creation, and He has a plan for your life. You don't need anybody else to be important or valued.

Question 3: I'm not into the stuff other guys (girls) are into. Does that mean I'm a homosexual?

Answer: In a word, no. Interests come and go over time. Do you still enjoy listening to the same music group you liked as a fifth grader? Probably not. Do you still play the same sport you did as a 10-year-old? Maybe, maybe not. Do you like the same colors, foods, or friends? Possibly. Or not. Interests, likes, dislikes, and hobbies change over time. They have nothing to do with homosexuality.

Sometimes the things you are into are shaped by the people around you. You may not dislike stuff other guys (girls) like, but you've never had the chance to learn about them. Guys, maybe you don't like football because when you were younger, your dad wasn't around to throw the ball or take you to games. Girls, you might prefer jeans and baseball because your mom spent a lot of time away on business and your dad and brothers took care of you.

If you think you might want to learn about "guy stuff" or "girl stuff," find adults in your church or community who could teach you about those things. They'd love to share their interests with you.

Question 4: I'm just not into the whole dating scene. Does that mean I'm a homosexual?

Answer: Just because you're not into dating doesn't mean you're a homosexual. For many teenagers, dating just takes too much time. Many teens choose to be involved in other activities—sports, clubs, hobbies, heavy class loads—that take up the bulk of their time, leaving little time for dating. One teen recently told me that he'd broken up with his girlfriend because he didn't have time for her. He was struggling with his grades, was involved with his church, and played on three different soccer teams (he wants to play professionally). For him the best option was to delay dating for a while. Strong, quality relationships take time and energy to grow—two things many teens just don't want to give up. Those teens are not homosexuals. They just know their limits.

Also keep in mind that you're going through a lot of changes as a teenager, and you may not have developed an attraction to the opposite sex yet. That attraction may not develop until later, but many teens feel pressured to date anyway. In fact, many teens date for the wrong reasons: shock, sexual release, to make their parents mad, or just to be "like everyone else." Don't be pressured into dating before you're ready. Just relax.

One last thought: You may not be dating because you're uncomfortable around the opposite gender. Guess what? That is completely normal. It's quite common to experience sweaty palms, to get tongue-tied and be unable to talk well, and to feel nervous when you're around someone to whom you're attracted. Don't let this discomfort alarm you or make you think something's wrong. Instead of dating that person exclusively, you may just want to hang out with a group of friends, both guys and girls. It'll give you the chance to become more comfortable with the opposite sex, and you'll learn how to relate better with them, too. Then, when you're more comfortable, you can begin to think about dating.

Question 5: I was sexually abused by a person of my own gender, but I got turned on. Does that mean I'm a homosexual?

Answer: What happened to you was wrong. It wasn't your fault. You didn't "ask" for it. You didn't deserve it. You're not bad, damaged, or used up. Something terrible happened to you, but you are not to blame. You didn't sin, and it doesn't mean you're a homosexual.

Many people, especially guys, are aroused by sexual abuse. Why? Because your body doesn't know whether it's being touched by a male or a female. It will automatically respond to pleasurable touch. It's like having the keys to your parent's car. The car doesn't know who's starting it—your parents (they have permission to drive the car), or you (you don't have permission to drive it). It just starts when the key is used. When someone touches you in a desirable area, such as your genitals, your body will respond automatically.[1]

If someone has sexually abused you, tell someone about what happened. Talk to your youth minister, pastor, teacher, or another caring adult. It'll take a lot of courage, but he or she can help you find a Christian counselor to talk through and deal with the trauma associated with sexual abuse.

Question 6: I have some homosexual feelings. Now what do I do?

Answer: First, don't panic. Don't do anything rash or impulsive. Don't automatically label yourself as a homosexual and dive into some behaviors you'd later regret. Second, take a look at your surroundings and actions. If you're spending all your time with homosexuals, their attitudes and behavior may be influencing yours. If you're viewing homosexual pornography on the Internet, you're feeding the feelings. Take a step back and evaluate why you might be experiencing some homosexual feelings. Third, talk to a trusted adult. You may feel comfortable talking with a youth minister or pastor. Talk with your parents. If you don't think you can talk to them, then contact a professional who specializes in this area. Listed on the next few pages are some organizations with personnel who would be willing to help you talk through your feelings. Keep in mind that you'll probably feel a little uncomfortable bringing up the subject up with anyone. That anxiety is normal. Don't let it stop you from getting some godly guidance and advice.

Question 7: If homosexuality isn't genetic, then what causes it?

Answer: Understanding the roots of homosexuality is a bit more complicated than understanding cause and effect. To say that homosexuality is caused by something implies that if you take that problem away, then homosexual feelings will be gone instantly. While there is no single reason people pursue homosexual relationships, often there are some common factors that lead to this behavior. (And knowing those factors can help the healing process.) Among people who tell their stories, three themes surface: sexual abuse, relationship with parents, and interaction with peers.[2] Sexual abuse is a large contributor to homosexuality. Not everyone who is the victim of sexual abuse becomes a homosexual; not everyone who is a homosexual was sexually abused. However, a large number of people involved in homosexuality were sexually abused at some point in their childhood. In fact, New Direction, a Canadian ministry to those who want to leave the homosexual lifestyle, indicates that 70 percent of those who seek help from them have been sexually abused.[3]

Sexual abuse teaches young girls that it's dangerous and painful to be with a man. And, in many cases, young girls learn that it's not OK to be a girl. To be a girl means being vulnerable, and they won't ever let that happen again, so they reject anything feminine. For guys, sexual abuse leaves them thinking that love is equated with a sexual encounter. Or they are ashamed because they were aroused during sexual abuse (which is very common). They assume that because they were aroused, they must be homosexual.

The parent relationship can also be a factor in homosexual behavior. For example, a boy may have a "father who is distant, detached, and hostile and a mother who is overly warm, possessive, and controlling . . . the boy's desire to identify with the father is frustrated, and the seeds of fear and a longing for closeness to a male are planted."[4] Or take the example of Teresa. Her father was emotionally abusive to the female members of her family, including her sister and her mother. Her mother could not stand up for herself or her daughters, and Teresa saw the wounds such abuse left on her family. Teresa learned early on to protect herself from the abuse of her father. In that process, she drew the conclusion that men in general could not be trusted and would not provide love.

Children who are rejected by their parents are sometimes rejected by their peers as well. This heaps on more confusion and insecurity. Guys may not feel like they "fit in" with the other guys, doing guy stuff like sports or cars. Girls may not feel pretty enough or confident enough to do "girl stuff." This rejection leads them to seek acceptance, even if the relationship isn't healthy.

Remember, homosexuality is not really about sexual encounters. Many people who engage in homosexuality are really struggling with a larger issue—loneliness, rejection, gender identity, self-hatred, or the need for affirmation, approval, and protection.[5]

Question 8: If I hang out with people who are homosexuals, won't people think I'm gay, too?

Answer:
Let's face it. There are some people who will assume you are "guilty by association." They're quick to judge and get into other people's business. Those people might label you a homosexual if you spend time with a friend who is a homosexual. Remember, though, that the people who love and care about you, who really know you, won't label you by your choice of friendships. You can either reach out to a friend who's struggling or spend time worrying about what other people think. You can't do both. Also keep in mind the ultimate Example. Jesus reached out to people who needed His love and didn't worry about what others said about Him. He knew people were more important than what others thought.

References

[1]"I think I'm a lesbian," *Free to Be Me* [online], 1999 [cited 4 December 2003]. Available from Internet: *www.freetobeme.com/iti_lesb.htm*

[2]Jeff Olson, "When Passions Are Confused," [online], cited 4 December 2003. Available from Internet: *www.gospelcom.net/rbc/ds/cb962/cb962.html#intro.*

[3]"Sexual abuse as a contributing factor: Expanding on the developmental view of

sexuality," *New Direction* [online], cited 4 December 2003. Available from Internet: *www.newdirection.ca/a_abuse.htm*

[4]Dr. Les Parrott III, *Helping Your Struggling Teenager* (Grand Rapids: Zondervan Publishing, 2000), 177.

[5]James Dobson, "Dr. Dobson's Study," *family.org* [online] June 2002 [cited 4 December 2003]. Available from Internet: *www.family.org/docstudy/newlsetters/a0021043.html.*

APPENDIX 2: Additional Resources

Books

The Heart of the Matter: Roots and Causes of Female Homosexuality

Anne Paulk and Jane Boyer, speakers and former lesbians, contribute to this book that explores the factors that contribute to homosexuality. It examines factors such as physical and emotional trauma, relationship with parents, and unhealthy family environment. It is available through Focus on the Family, *www.family.org.*

Straight Answers: Exposing the Myths and Facts About Homosexuality by Mike Haley

This book discusses eight of the most common myths surrounding homosexuality, dealing with questions such as: Are homosexuals born gay? Does the Bible really condemn homosexuality? It is available through Focus on the Family, *www.family.org.*

Dark Obsession by Timothy J. Dailey

This book chronicles the devastating effects of homosexuality on one man, his family, and his friendships. It is also a discussion of homosexuality from a biblical perspective. It provides information about cultural arguments regarding homosexuality, the negative health effects of homosexuality, and many other related issues.

Love Won Out by John and Anne Paulk

This book tells the story of how God's love helped two people escape the bondage of homosexuality and eventually find each other. This true account about two people who lived in different places but shared the same struggle of homosexuality tells how God's tender love transformed their lives. This story is a source of hope, proving again that homosexuals can change by the power of God's love.

Coming Out of Homosexuality by Bob Davies and Lori Rentzel
This book is a practical guide for people struggling with homosexuality. It contains discussions on the dynamics of change, exposing the roots of homosexual attraction, breaking addictive patterns, and forming healthy friendships.

Someone I Love Is Gay by Anita Worthen and Bob Davies
This book is geared toward helping you respond to a gay friend or relative in a loving and nonjudgmental manner. It will help you understand your own emotions and will provide answers for you and your friend or family member.

Christian Ministries

Exodus International is a group of churches, counselors, and other individuals who want to offer help and support to men and women who want to overcome homosexuality. They offer support groups, counseling, literature, and other resources. Their Web site is listed below. You can also contact them by calling 206-784-7799 or writing to PO BOX 77652, Seattle, WA 98177.

National Association for Research and Therapy of Homosexuality (NARTH) offers an international referral service of licensed therapists, research on the factors leading to homosexuality, lectures by respected mental health professionals, information for the general public, and literature distribution into college, high school, and community libraries. Their Web site is listed below. You can also contact NARTH by calling 818-789-4440 or by writing to 16633 Ventura Boulevard, Suite 1340, Encino, CA 91436-1801.

Focus on the Family is a nonprofit organization that seeks to preserve biblical values and the institution of the family. Focus provides information and education concerning a wide range of issues, including homosexuality. They offer educational materials including books, pamphlets, and video and audio tapes. This organization also hosts a one-day seminar on the subject of homosexuality. Information about this seminar, "Love Won Out," can be found on the Web site listed below. You can contact Focus on the Family by calling 1-800-A-FAMILY or by writing to Focus on the Family, Colorado Springs, CO 80995.

New Direction for Life Ministries is a Canadian organization that helps men and women who choose to leave homosexuality while respecting those who make other choices. They offer Christian support to men and women choosing to leave homosexuality and seek to equip the church to minister to people struggling with this issue. Their Web sites for teens are listed below.

Web Sites

The following Web sites contain information about the biblical perspective of homosexuality. Whether you're personally struggling with homosexual attractions or just want more information, these Web sites are a great place to look.

- Exodus International—*www.exodus-international.org*
- Exodus International for teenagers—*www.exodusyouth.net*
- Focus on the Family—*www.family.org*
- Free to Be Me (in connection with New Direction)—*www.freetobeme.com*
- Becoming Real (in connection with New Direction)—*www.becomingreal.org*
- NARTH—*www.narth.com*

GROUP STUDY
Teaching Plans

The following pages contain teaching plans for youth leaders who choose to use *Designed by God* as a group study. Each week will focus on answering the question posed in each chapter of the book. Make sure to stay focused on that one question; don't get ahead of yourself and overlap sessions.

The study provides an opening activity to get students' attention and guided discovery activities geared for group work. If you have a small group of students, you can group into pairs or assign work to one person. Also, a page for notes is provided at the end of each teaching plan. Use this to jot down further thoughts, additional teaching ideas, or other preparations such as room setup. Also keep in mind that you may need to do some preparation prior to the lesson. Each lesson lists supplies and resources that will need to be gathered or prepared before the study.

Here are some important things to keep in mind if you choose to complete *Designed by God* as a group study.

Read the book yourself before teaching it.
Because you will be summarizing information from this book, it will be helpful for you to read the book yourself first. Also, chapter 3 discusses scientific studies that contain medical jargon. By reading the book prior to the study, you can absorb that material to explain it to students who may not readily understand it.

Maintain a positive atmosphere.
Do not allow negative comments, inappropriate jokes, or snide remarks. Students who are struggling with this issue may be

among the ones who attend this study. If you allow prejudicial remarks or off-color comments, you communicate a lack of respect for this subject. You may also drive away a student who is searching for love and answers. As a leader, you set the atmosphere, so make sure the atmosphere is positive.

Provide a book for each student.

While you may be tempted just to use one book to teach the information, students will gain more insight if they can read and digest the information on their own. The book contains response spaces; using those sections will help students who learn by writing. Also, many students will not ask questions during the Bible study, but by having their own copy of the book, they can refer to it later or go to one of the Web sites listed to get more information.

Take time each week to examine one of the "Questions Teenagers Ask" in Appendix A.

At the end of each Bible study, take time to read and discuss one of the questions. As an option, you could take one more week to cover the material in Appendix A. However, students may not want to wait several weeks to have the unvoiced questions answered, so discussing one each week may help a student who is really wrestling with some tough questions.

Be willing to spend more than one week on a chapter if necessary.

If you find that a chapter cannot be covered adequately in one session, take more time with it. This is especially true in Chapter 3 and Chapter 4. Both cover a large amount of material that may be difficult for some students to grasp in just an hour. You may need to break the chapters into smaller chunks and deal with those sections over a couple of weeks. It's more important for students to understand the truth and articulate it than to cover the material in a shorter time frame.

CHAPTER 1: ORIGINAL DESIGN

Overview

In this session students will learn how God designed men and women to relate to each other.

Supplies and Resources

Opening: Poster board, markers, newspaper and magazine articles if possible
Design Is Everywhere: *Designed by God* books, pens or pencils
Created to Relate: Paper for teams

Opening

As teens arrive, direct them to list on poster board things they've heard about homosexuality. Guide them to list TV shows, movies, music, and magazines that deal with homosexuality. (If you have a large number of students, group them into teams for this assignment.) After everyone has had a chance to contribute, review the students' answers. Then say: **Homosexuality is a big topic in our world today.** Ask: **What are some questions you have about homosexuality?** Review the six questions that will be answered over the next few weeks. Say: **Today, we'll focus on the first question to discover how God designed our sexuality.**

Design Is Everywhere

Summarize the information on page 7 of the student book under "Design Is Everywhere." Ask: **As you look around the room, what things have a specific design?** Say: **Let's learn about God's design for our sexuality.**

Distribute *Designed by God* books. Direct teens to complete the section "Back to the Beginning—Created Male and Female" on pages 8-9. After several minutes, review their responses, allowing time for students to ask questions. Then ask: **What does this passage tell us about our design as human beings?** (refer to page 9 if necessary) **How do you feel knowing that God created men and women differently? How have you seen or experienced the differences between men and women? Do you like being created differently from the opposite gender? Why or why not?**

Back to the Bible—Created to Relate

Group students into two teams by gender. Direct teams to complete the section "Back to the Beginning—Created to Relate" on pages 10-11. Direct teams to create a monologue from the perspective of Adam based on the information they have gathered from their group study. After several minutes, allow both teams to present their monologues. Then ask the following questions: **Why do you think God created Eve from Adam's rib? How do you think Adam felt before Eve was created? Why did God create Eve? Why weren't animals suitable helpers for Adam? Why didn't God just create another man to be a friend to Adam? What does this say about God's love for you and me? How do you think Adam felt after God created Eve?** Guide students to recognize that when God created Eve, He set forth the framework for biblical sexuality: between one man and one woman within the boundaries of marriage. Help them to recognize that God didn't create another male as a helper. Instead, He created a woman, someone distinctly different from Adam.

Putting It All Together

Ask: **How does this understanding of our sexuality differ from what our culture tells us? Do you think this viewpoint is very popular in our culture? Why or why not?** As a group, discuss how teens can celebrate being created by God in a unique and purposeful way. Ask: **If that was God's design, what happened?** Then say: **Next week we'll discover what happened to God's plan for human sexuality.** Spend a few minutes discussing one of the questions students ask in Appendix A. Close in prayer.

CHAPTER 2: THE FALL

Overview
In this session students will learn what happened to God's plan for human sexuality.

Supplies and Resources
Opening: magazines, newspapers
The Story Unfolds: *Designed by God* books, pens or pencils
Equal Footing: Paper

Opening
As teens arrive, direct them to look through magazines and newspapers for examples of sin. Lead teens to tear out the examples. Call on students to share their examples. Then ask: **Where did sin come from?** Say: **Today we'll discover what happened to God's plan for sexuality. The effects of sin are far-reaching.**

The Story Unfolds
Group teens into pairs. Distribute *Designed by God* books and instruct pairs to complete the activity on pages 15-16. After several minutes, review the events, placing them in order. Then lead out in discussion, asking: **What happened when Adam and Eve ate the fruit? What did they realize? When God came looking for Adam and Eve, what did they do? How did God respond to them? How do you think God felt when Adam and Eve rebelled against Him? How does this discussion of humanity's first sin relate to homosexuality?** Use the information on page 18 to enhance discussion. Then say: **We know where sin came from. Sin entered the picture with Adam and Eve, and we still feel its effects. One of those sins is homosexuality, when people choose to go outside God's plan for their sexuality. Before we begin to think of homosexuals as bad people, let's look at our own lives for a minute.**

Bad News, Good News (Supplemental Option)

If you have several teens who are not believers, explain how to become a believer. Use the Scriptures, questions, and information on pages 21-23 for help. Then continue with the activities below.

Equal Footing

Direct teens to look back over the examples of sin they found in the magazines during the opening activity. Direct youth to rate those sins according to their severity, then post them on the wall, ranging from "worst" to "not really bad." Don't provide any more direction to the students. Let them wrestle with where to place their examples. Ask: **How easy was this process? Why? Do you think God views our sin that way? Why or why not?** (Briefly tell the skyscraper illustration on page 23 to illustrate how God views sin.) **Do you think people view the sin of homosexuality as worse than other sins? Why? If God doesn't grade sin, why do we?**

Call on a teen to read John 8:1-11. Distribute paper and pens and direct teens to write what the woman might have been thinking, feeling, hearing, or even smelling as the events in this story unfold. Call on teens to share their answers. Then ask: **Which of the characters are you most like: the teacher of the law, the woman caught in sin, or Jesus, who extended grace?** Explain that sin is sin. Say: **There's no measurement to it, no ranking from really big to minor. Anything that rebels against God's commands is a sin. It's true that different sins carry different consequences, but all sin breaks God's heart.** Use the information on page 26 to highlight God's love for people despite their sin.

Spend a few minutes discussing one of the questions students ask in Appendix A. Close with a time of silent prayer, challenging students to think about what their lives would be like if Jesus had not demonstrated mercy and love toward them. Challenge them to begin to evaluate how they respond to people who are different from them.

CHAPTER 3: A LOUD VOICE

Overview

In this session students will evaluate what culture says about homosexuality.

Supplies and Resources

The Number One Message: Large sheet of paper, markers

Opening

To open, group teens in the center of the room. Explain that you will read several stories and they will determine whether each story is factual or an urban legend. (You may need to explain what an urban legend is, using information from the book.) Designate two opposite sides of the room as Urban Legend and Factual Story. Read each of the stories or statements on page 30. Give teens a chance to vote by standing on the appropriate side of the room. Then call on several students to explain why they thought the story was either fact or fiction. Then ask: **Why are people quick to believe an urban legend? What makes an urban legend believable?** Use the information on page 31 to explain how people are quick to believe something without checking out the facts. Then say: **Today we'll discuss some things culture says about homosexuality. We'll see that the "facts" culture presents aren't so factual.**

The Number One Message

Group students into three teams. Explain that one of the major claims of culture is that homosexuality is genetic or biological. Explain that each team will evaluate a scientific study used to support this genetic argument. Give teams the following assignments: **Team 1:** "The X Chromosome Study," pages 32-33; **Team 2:** "The Twin Study," pages 34-35 **Team 3:** "The Hypothalamus Study," pages 36-37. Direct all teams to answer the same questions: *What was the subject of the study? (body part, chromosome, etc.) What* *were the results of the study? What conclusions were made as a result of the study? What problems were found in the study?* As teams are working on their assignments, tape a large sheet of paper to a focal wall and create four columns: *Subject, Results, Conclusions, Problems.* Down the left side of the paper, create three sections: *X Chromosome Study; Twin Study; Hypothalamus Study.*

Direct teams to present their information. List their findings on the chart you created. After each group shares, provide supplemental information as necessary. After all teams have provided their summaries, ask: **Is this new information to you? Why do you think you don't hear about the problems with these studies?** Then summarize the section "Genetics Versus Behavior" on page 37. Help students recognize that every person has a sinful nature, but sinful nature doesn't excuse behavior.

Ask: **Do you think homosexual behavior can be changed?** Allow for responses. Then share the story of John and Anne found on page 39. Then call on a student to read 1 Corinthians 6:9-11. Ask: **What is one word in this passage that tells us whether homosexuality can be changed?** Say: **A key word in this passage is the word *were*. Paul wrote to some people who had been homosexuals but had since changed through God's help. This tells us that homosexuality can be changed.**

Say: **One more statement culture makes is that 10 percent of the population is homosexual. They argue that if that many people are homosexual, then it can't be wrong.** Ask: **Is there a problem with this statement? Explain.** Using the information from pages 40-41, point out the problems with this argument. Ask: **Why do you think culture is so vocal in support of homosexuality? What's wrong with believing what culture tells us?** Then say: **Our standard of right and wrong is the Bible, not the world around us. Next week, we'll discover what the Bible really says about homosexuality.** Spend a few minutes discussing one of the questions students ask in Appendix A.

CHAPTER 4: AN AUTHORITATIVE WORD

Overview
In this session students will discover what the Bible says about homosexuality.

Supplies and Resources
Opening: Prepared true/false quiz, pens
Group Work: poster board, markers

Opening
Prior to the lesson, create and make copies of a true/false test of general knowledge about the Bible. Include statements such as: *The Bible says God helps those who help themselves* and *Hezekiah is a book in the Bible*. Be sure to include a statement that says: *The Bible calls homosexuality a sin*. As students arrive, distribute the test and instruct teens to complete it. After most teens have arrived, review the quiz and give a prize to the teen with the most correct answers. Then say: **Sometimes we get our Bible facts mixed up. Today we'll discover what God's Word says about homosexuality.**

Group Work
Group students into four teams and assign teams the following Scripture passages and pages in *Designed by God*:
Team 1: Leviticus 18:22; 20:13 and pages 49-52
Team 2: Romans 1:24-28 and pages 52-54
Team 3: 1 Corinthians 6:9-11 and pages 54-56
Team 4: "One Last Argument" on page 56
Distribute poster board and markers to teams. Direct teams to read their assigned portions and to create a headline based on what homosexual activists would say about that passage of Scripture. Also direct teams to be prepared to explain why this statement is false.

After several minutes, call on Team 1 to present its headline. Also direct the team to indicate why that headline is inaccurate. Spend a few minutes explaining the background of Leviticus. Ask: **Does this help you understand Leviticus more? Why or why not? Which aspects of Leviticus still apply to believers today?**

Call on Team 2 to read its Scripture, present its headline, and explain why the headline is false. Then ask: **What do you think would happen if every person did what came natural to them? What's wrong with thinking that any behavior is OK as long as it's done "in love"?**

Call on Team 3 and Team 4 to present their information. Ask: **How can God be the author of Scripture if men actually wrote the Bible?** (God inspired or led people to write.) **Why is it important to remember that God is the author of Scripture? Why is it dangerous to ignore Scripture that the human writers might not have completely understood?** To help students review what they've learned, direct them to complete the case studies on pages 57-58. Give teens a chance to address each of the case studies.

Other Thing∫ People ∫ay

To help students know how to respond to other arguments people make in defense of homosexuality, read each of the statements on page 58-59. After each statement, give teens the opportunity to share what they might say in response. Encourage teens to write down other students' response. If no one gives a response, use the prepared responses provided on pages 59-61.

Spend a few minutes discussing one of the questions students ask in Appendix A. Then close in prayer. Ask God to guide students to hold to the truth of Scripture even though it may mean being disliked or labeled as intolerant.

CHAPTER 5: BEING THERE

Overview

In this session students will discover how to help a friend who's struggling with homosexuality.

Supplies and Resources

Opening: poster board, markers for each team
Practical Points: paper, markers for each team

Opening

As teens arrive, group them into teams and supply each team with poster board and markers. Direct teams to create a Top 10 list of the worst things to say or do for a friend who's going through a hard time. Challenge them to be creative but tasteful in their lists. Call on teams to present their lists. Highlight important principles teens uncover, such as listening to friends or asking for adult help. Then say: **Today we'll discover how to help friends who may be struggling with homosexuality.**

Prime Examples

Say: **Before we look at principles for helping a struggling friend, let's see how Jesus responded to people in trouble.** Group teens into two teams and assign one team Luke 10:25-32 and the other team Luke 5:27-32. Direct teams to act out the stories found in their passages. (If you have a large group, break teens into smaller teams and assign the Scriptures to multiple groups.) After several minutes, call on the first team to act out its skit. After the story, challenge teens to recall what each character did. Review the information on pages 66-67 with students, summarizing the story, and pointing out Jesus' emphasis of loving others. Ask: **How does this story relate to our study of homosexuality?** After teens have responded, direct them to complete the activity on pages 67-68, identifying the character in the story they are most like. Allow teens to share their responses as they feel comfortable. Then call on the other team to share its skit. After the skit, ask: **Who was involved in the conflict? How did Jesus respond? Why do you think He responded this way?** Summarize the information on pages 70-72, helping students recognize the need to love people while holding to the truth of Scripture. Then say: **Now that we've learned how Jesus commanded us to relate to others in need, let's look at some specific principles for helping people who have questions about homosexuality.**

Practical Points

Group students into 10 teams. (One person can be a team or can be assigned more than one Scripture.) Assign each team one of the "Practical Points" found on pages 73-78. Provide paper and markers. Direct teens to read the practical point assigned and to create a bumper sticker that summarizes the information. Call on the first team to display its bumper sticker and explain point 1. Repeat this process for teams 2 through 10. Direct the subsequent teams to display their bumper sticker next to the first one, creating a list of positive principles for relating to people who have questions or struggles with homosexuality. Ask: **Which of these principles would be the easiest to put into practice? Which of these principles would be the most difficult to put into practice?**

Putting It All Together

Direct teens to read each of the case studies found on pages 79-81 and to record how they would respond. Review the case studies, highlighting the principles you learned together. Allow teens to ask questions. To close the session, point out "P.S. Some Things Not to Say" on pages 81-82 and discuss why those statements would not be helpful. Then ask: **What's one principle you've learned today that you can put into practice this week?** Spend a few minutes discussing one of the questions students ask in Appendix A. Then close in prayer, asking God to guide students to help others in need.

CHAPTER 6: A SOLID FOUNDATION

Overview

In this session teens will discover how to develop healthy relationships. They will also identify warning signs of an unhealthy relationship.

Supplies and Resources

Opening: Prepared signs, markers, tape

Opening

Prior to the lesson, write the following on large sheets of paper and tape them around the room: *Warning signs of a hurricane; Warning signs of a cold; Warning signs of a breakup; Warning signs of a heart attack; Warning signs of being fired; Warning signs of road work ahead.* As students arrive, distribute markers and instruct teens to list the warning signs for each of the categories listed. Review their answers. Then say: **Just as there are warning signs for a hurricane or a heart attack, there are also warning signs for unhealthy relationships. Today we'll learn about those signs, as well as the signs of healthy relationships.**

Friendship in the Bible

Say: **Let's see what the Bible says about healthy relationships.** Group teens into eight teams and assign teams one of the Scriptures listed on page 88. (One person can be a team, or teams could deal with multiple Scripture passages.) Direct teams to read their assigned verse(s) and discover the characteristic of a good friend. Also direct them to provide a practical example of that characteristic. After several minutes, call on the first team to read its Scripture and share the principle and practical example. Direct teens to record those answers on page 88 as indicated. Then review with teens the information on page 87 as it related to that particular principle. Also direct teens to answer the question under Principle 1. Repeat this process for the other Scriptures. After all teams have shared, direct teens to complete the evaluation chart on page 94. Challenge teens to think honestly about their relationships. Then as time allows, discuss other characteristics of a healthy relationship. Use the information on pages 93-95 to spark discussion. Be sure to highlight the importance of boundaries and appropriate physical touch, as some students may have been in unhealthy or abusive relationships. Then say: **Let's look at some warning signs of unhealthy relationships.**

Signs of Unhealthy Relationships

Prior to the lesson, scramble the words for each unhealthy characteristic listed on pages 96 and write the scrambled words on a large sheet of paper or chalkboard. Instruct teens to work together to unscramble the unhealthy characteristics. As each one is unscrambled, discuss it briefly. Then say: **Now that you've learned characteristics of healthy and unhealthy relationships, let's test your knowledge.** Group teens into four groups and assign each group to one of the case studies on pages 97-98. Direct them to evaluate whether each friendship is healthy and to indicate the reason for their choices. After several minutes, call on teams to share their case studies, their responses, and the reason they labeled the relationship healthy or unhealthy. Then direct teens to complete "Write Your Own Story" on page 98. Give teens the opportunity to share their stories.

Review one of the questions teenagers ask in Appendix A. Also, point out the list of resources found in Appendix B. Let students know that you're willing to talk with them about questions or problems they or someone else may be having in dealing with homosexuality. Be sure to maintain sensitivity and compassion. Close the session in prayer.